68.00

I0742418

ECONOMIC FREEDOM

AND HUMAN FLOURISHING

PERSPECTIVES FROM POLITICAL PHILOSOPHY

Steven Bilakovics • Richard Boyd
Ryan Patrick Hanley • Peter B. Josephson
Yuval Levin • Harvey C. Mansfield
Deirdre Nansen McCloskey • John T. Scott
Susan Meld Shell

Edited by Michael R. Strain and Stan A. Veuger

AMERICAN ENTERPRISE INSTITUTE

ISBN-13: 978-0-8447-5001-9 (hardback)
ISBN-10: 0-8447-5001-8 (hardback)
ISBN-13: 978-0-8447-5002-6 (paperback)
ISBN-10: 0-8447-5002-6 (paperback)
ISBN-13: 978-0-8447-5003-3 (ebook)
ISBN-10: 0-8447-5003-4 (ebook)

American Enterprise Institute
1150 17th St. NW
Washington, DC 20036
www.aei.org

Contents

iii

Preface

It is easy to forget the broader context in which public policy is placed. So much attention is paid to the means by which policy is conceived and implemented—politics—that it is easy to focus on the game and to lose sight of the reason the game exists in the first place. Conversely, in the world of public policy research, your view can easily become dominated by minutia: Is a particular elasticity equal to –0.1 or –0.2? Should a tax credit be capped at $500 per year or $750?

It is helpful and refreshing to broaden the lens from time to time. This collection seeks to do that.

Our subject is whether economic liberty is necessary for individuals to lead truly flourishing lives. This question underlies—or, at least, it should underlie—many of our most important policy debates. But it is harder to answer than it may seem. What do we mean by liberty? What is the flourishing life? And once settled on definitions, how are the two related?

To answer these questions, we rely on some of history's greatest thinkers, interpreted by some of today's leading scholars of their thought. Their essays are valuable—it turns out that Aristotle and Burke and Mill, and philosophers in their class, have much to offer today's public debate. And we still have much to learn from Marx's mistakes as well.

Politics is important. A deeper understanding of technical questions of economics and social science are important. Both are critical, even. But so too is an understanding of why these endeavors matter—or even exist.

M.R.S. & S.A.V.
Washington, DC
June 2016

Aristotle on Economics and the Flourishing Life

HARVEY C. MANSFIELD
Harvard University and the Hoover Institution

To introduce this large topic, it is fitting to consider Aristotle, for centuries "the master of those who know" (as Dante called him). By contrast to our thinking, Aristotle wrote comprehensively on both economics and the flourishing life. Modern economics makes its way without study of the "flourishing life," which is one translation of what Aristotle meant by happiness. For him, as for common sense, happiness is the goal of ethics and politics, and ultimately of economics. At present, however, economics contents itself with the "pursuit of happiness" (to borrow from the Declaration of Independence), a catchall category that specifies at great length how to pursue but hardly at all what to pursue.

If we follow Aristotle's method of beginning from what is familiar, we must begin from modern economics, which is more familiar to us than Aristotle. Every college student has taken, or should have taken, Economics 101, and those who have been deprived of this advantage have to learn what is taught in that course, perhaps more cheaply, perhaps not, in the School of Hard Knocks. Whether the study of economics is worth its cost is an example of a typical economic calculation, for economics is about calculation. A calculation is a deliberation that focuses on a number, a "metric," of more, of a greater quantity. It avoids the question of how much more is needed before one can decide that one can stop acquiring and turn to enjoyment. Originally—and this is in Aristotle as well as in the founders of modern economics—economics supposed that it could define needs or necessities as opposed to surplus or superfluities. But necessities have a way of expanding from survival to comfort and from comfort to perfect assurance, so that it seems safer, and scientifically more exact, to consider them infinite and thus decline to define them.

Economics becomes the science of getting more without ever saying how much more. It is because of its exactness that science requires this vagueness. Economics must either be exact or fall silent; it disdains and rejects the possibility of an inexact statement that is merely probable and better than nothing. It may attempt to evade the difficulty by defining "probability" exactly. The result would be either a vague definition of exact or an exact definition of vague— which leaves the common sense "probable" in charge. So the science of more, of "growth," drops the utilitarian posture that requires a definition of utility—possibly contestable—and turns to "preferences" that are admittedly quite subjective. Thus does the objectivity of economics require that it surrender totally to human subjectivity. And as the measuring of preferences becomes increasingly sophisticated, which means increasingly mathematical, economics becomes increasingly vague as to its end and continually further from defining the "flourishing life."

At the same time the boundary of economics becomes increasingly uncertain. It used to be that economists, when pressured with a question hard to answer, would frequently resort to a boundary statement and say: "That's a noneconomic question." That distinguished an economist from a political scientist, who could never say "that's a nonpolitical question" because politics admits no sanctuary from politics. But now economists have invaded political science, for example with game theory, reducing political questions to economic ones, and with the same increasing exactness that promotes increasing vagueness. It is true that many political scientists today, as distinguished from Aristotle, welcome these invaders as saviors of their science.

The discussion so far has a skeptical tone you will not find in Economics 101. But perhaps economics does have, despite its scientific pretensions, an end in view—and thus a contribution to the question of what is happiness. My father, a professor, used to rent his house in the summer to other professors who needed to live in the city he wanted to leave. This was an economic transaction. But he soon learned from hard experience that it was far preferable to rent to an economist than to a sociologist. His lesson was that economists believe in bourgeois virtue and sociologists do not. This is not a matter of calculation but of difference of habit, even of way of life, that he observed. Or it was calculation over the long term, never actually tested, that unkept promises and slovenly behavior would eventually be punished in this world: this is calculation not much different from virtue.

A problem of how to live can be seen within economic calculation. Which is better, to spend or to save? In the recent economic crisis, the American government passed a "stimulus" bill, meaning a stimulus on the consumer to spend. But it could also be said that in difficult times it is better to save—as many people did, not responding to the stimulus. Economic calculation might say that it is better sometimes to save, sometimes to spend, that to be rational one should have no predisposition for one or the other. But to spend or to save is a life choice; each way has habits of its own that are hard to change quickly in accordance with calculation, as when buying or selling a stock. A calculator is always ready to adjust and finds habit, which is fixed and not calculated, to be irrational (as in a way it is). Here, within economic rationality, we see two opposing ways of life, two opposite souls, the easy spender and the tightwad, both economic, but not determined solely by economic advantage.

Turning to Aristotle, we see him considering ways of life with a view to which is best rather than calculation of what brings in more. More what, he wants to know, and how much more? For him the "pursuit" of happiness implies an end to the pursuit, since endless pursuit is futile and irrational. All human beings pursue happiness; everything else is instrumental to happiness and pursued because it brings happiness. Even virtue, though an end in itself and often involving sacrifice, is also pursued as the means to happiness. Virtue won't, or at least shouldn't, make you miserable, Aristotle says, somewhat optimistically. To be happy is to be at rest, as we say, "sitting pretty." Those who scramble without end don't know how to stop, don't know how to enjoy. "Enjoy!" we say today in moments of respite; Aristotle would say that enjoyment (not relaxation) is the whole purpose of scrambling to get ahead. Relaxation is to gain respite from scrambling so that one can resume it refreshed, but enjoyment is satisfaction in an end attained.

The art or science of achieving happiness is political, and Aristotle calls politics the "master science," the one that orders and rules over all other sciences, arts, and practices in a society. Even a free society is ruled in such a way that its parts are free and contribute to the whole of a free society. The "free market" studied and recommended by economics has to be the result of a political decision to establish and maintain it. In general, only politics can restrain politics. The free market needs to be sustained by "bourgeois virtue" taught in the schools and the family in consequence of a fundamentally political decision to lead a certain way of life and to live by its rules. The indispensable lessons of Economics 101 also need to be taught by the permission and favor of politics. What we call "civil society" similarly needs the good opinion and sponsorship of our rulers. Under the notion of "rule" Aristotle puts the main principles or principle of every way of life, so that politics promotes a definition of happiness, not just the means to undefined happiness. "Pluralism" in a society establishes a pluralistic society, a certain type of society distinctive in its ways from other, more prescriptive societies that it rejects and excludes. Aristotle's "master science" provides a comprehensive role for politics, but it should not be confused with a program for Big Government.

Reading from Aristotle's *Ethics* as well as his *Politics*, we see he maintains that virtue is the core of happiness. He means this in both a normative and a descriptive sense. Descriptively, every society has a virtue or cluster of virtues that it promotes as characterizing its way of life and defining its notion of happiness, often in his day the virtue of courage or martial spirit. But as every society claims that its prized virtue is best, Aristotle feels bound to judge normatively whether this claim is correct. For him there is no unbridgeable distinction between fact and value.

Now it is obvious that virtue cannot assure happiness. This is true not so much because we often witness the sad fact of virtue unrewarded—for virtue is its own reward (not always sufficient!)—but because we observe virtue thwarted for lack of means. Virtue stands in need of "equipment," Aristotle says nicely. It needs good fortune or the gods' blessing (implied in the Greek word for happiness, *eudaimonia*, well-blessed), and it needs wealth. One cannot be generous without wealth to give away. Here enters the need for economics as akin to a science of wealth-getting but distinct from it because economics needs to be limited. Aristotle does not hold to the purity of virtue understood as bringing no personal advantage (called "altruism"), but he does agree that wealth-getting is morally dangerous. It is essentially instrumental to virtue but can often become an end in itself regardless of virtue, Aristotle here in accord with Karl Marx. Money monetizes everything, as with the touch of King Midas, and thereby seems to dissolve all value except itself.

Virtue as the core of happiness is a habit, not a calculation. If you have to calculate the advantage from virtue, you are no longer being virtuous for the sake of virtue, which is no longer virtuous. You are merely behaving virtuously while others are watching, which is not enough. Virtue is in the intent as well as in the action. Yet again Aristotle admits that calculation can enter into virtue, for example, a generous person calculating how much to give or a courageous person reasoning in a situation of combat so as to avoid being rash. Virtue is divided into virtues, of which Aristotle names 11. An individual can practice one virtue without the others, and although it is desirable to have all the virtues, and Aristotle adds, to know you have them, this is rare.

Like individuals, societies (or, since "society" is a modern construct, political regimes, *politeiai*) tend to specialize in certain virtues. Indeed, regimes are necessarily biased in a certain direction, whereas a rare individual might have all the virtues. Regimes have laws that enshrine their characteristic virtues and make it difficult to adjust to new situations as they might do if they were more calculating. Most men and hence all peoples, because they have a character or type, resist change until they are compelled to change, and then they adopt and hold to the new regime. One revolution leads in time to another, not to an end of revolution—even though all revolution aims at being the final revolution. In the long view politics must recognize the limits to what can be achieved by politics, which means by human beings. The indefinite or infinite growth that modern economics dimly imagines as its goal is not viable, even if "growth" into nothing definite were intelligible as mere expansion. The same goes for the modern notion of progress or perfectibility, which today has dissolved into "change," as if it were possible for change to occur except with respect to something that does not change. For if "America has changed totally," how could you still call it "America"?

Within Aristotelian virtue there is a distinction characteristic of the Socratic tradition and very important for both economics and flourishing life. This is between the just and the noble. The just is what can be expected from citizens, one's duty or obligation; it contains an element of compulsion although it is voluntary like all the virtues. Examples are paying one's taxes or bills; payment is virtuous but expected and therefore not admired. Noble actions, however, go "beyond the call of duty," as we still say; they contain an element of risk and might earn a medal. Modern morality dating from Thomas Hobbes wants to avoid this distinction and to make all morality more certain by considering all of it (typically) under the concept of justice as virtue to be expected. This move permits all morality to be more predictable and calculable, less subject to chance. Happiness in a flourishing life may be more attractive, more admirable, as in the classical gentleman, but *homo economicus*—the morality of man subject to the laws of economics—is more regular and dependable.

The morality of the modern economic man can be calculated together with his economic behavior. In this calculation another distinction within Aristotelian virtue between intellectual and moral virtue can be overcome and the two combined. In the modern view, moral virtue comes under the rule of theory instead of being distinct from it. Moral theory takes the place of ordinary, unscientific praise and blame, and modern philosophers no longer make a point of rising above morality but stoop down to take charge of it. Happiness is regularized by being reduced to something less than the flourishing life of a gentleman or lady, let alone a philosopher—to a more attainable life such as bourgeois virtue. Bourgeois virtue has not been an unqualified success, however. It turns out that the morality that is more easily attained is also less satisfying, less interesting. A new concern for the boredom of bourgeois society arises, and *ennui* becomes the problem. Sociology with its critique of bourgeois happiness is born. Modern man would rather be "inner-directed" toward self-expression than calculate his self-interest in conformity with society's norms. A version or perversion of ancient nobility comes to life again in the guise of the radical and the hippy, who in their separate lives concur to disdain the pettiness of bourgeois virtue.

Of the two parts of Aristotle's virtue, the noble is more a problem for economics. The noble makes us resist economic advantage and the insistence of "incentives" (another modern concept). We often refuse what is presented to us as necessity when necessity no longer seems truly necessary. Economics expands necessity from minimum survival to the necessity of seeking a return on one's money. The rich man cannot afford not to exploit the opportunities he sees. The poor and their advocates will question this sort of "necessity." Also, what makes virtue noble is doing it for its own sake rather than for your private advantage. Yet Aristotle, still eschewing moral purity, says that virtue is for your advantage as well. Virtue makes you a better person, and perhaps a still better person if you realize that your virtue makes you better. For virtue is enhanced when aware of itself as the best kind of enjoyment. Similarly, the virtuous person does not seek pleasure, but he gets pleasure as a by-product of his virtue, taking a moderate pleasure in doing good and avoiding too much self-congratulation or superiority.

What is a better person? It is one with a better soul. Aristotle's moral, political, and economic thought is based on the soul. In the best case the soul is well-ordered and harmonious, but in every case the soul is a human being's individual self-government. The soul enables the individual to act and to reflect for himself, as opposed to the various determinants by which we are known and controlled by the various modern sciences, all of them denying or overlooking the soul. Hovering over us today, these sciences want to run our lives for us through the laws peculiar to each of them: laws of psychology, biology, chemistry, neurology, and—not least—economics.

Much of today's political science, soulless but not selfless, tries to imitate these more pretentious and more successful sciences. The soul, which Aristotle studied so well, stands in the way of these types of enslavement. It represents freedom in its various aspects: the freedom to resist necessity and nature (a freedom given to us by nature), the freedom to initiate action, the freedom to stop and reflect, the freedom to take satisfaction in oneself, and the freedom to blame oneself and feel shame. Human beings with souls fall in love and feel anger—two types of action that a calculating person never does and that the calculating sciences never know of.

We need a return to reason, to Aristotelian reason. The reason of economics is not empirical as it claims. It is based on the dubious presumption that human beings suffer in a condition of scarcity or necessity that will oblige them with their "preferences" (really, their necessities) to choose in ways that economists can predict and then control. This sort of reason begins in a dubious presumption that denies human freedom, and it dissolves, we have seen, in vagueness that fails to specify a reasonable goal of human life. Aristotle's reason, by contrast, admits human necessities, for he was one of the founders of economics. But, because it is more empirical than economics by itself on the basis of human experience, it also seeks, through the soul, to come to terms with human nobility and freedom. Aristotle's reason does its best to define the flourishing life, at its peak as well as in average, and measure the ordinary and the common by what is best and rare.

Hobbes, Locke, and the Problems of Political Economy

PETER B. JOSEPHSON
Saint Anselm College

In our own time and place we hotly contest the relation of public and private goods or interests. Education, health and birth control, energy and the environment, transportation, social welfare—almost any domestic issue is the subject of such debate. Those debates typically contest whether the issue at hand is properly a matter of public policy at all, and if it is, whether the best approach to addressing the concern is through public or private action. The contest over what is properly a public concern and what is properly private, and therefore over the extent of government authority and the defense of personal responsibility and liberty, has a long history in America. It is a legacy from our founding and from the intellectual origins of the founding. Those original intellects often thought better about these enduring problems than we typically do today. Thus we can better understand our own debate by considering its intellectual roots in the revolutionary political theories of 17th century England, and the understanding in that time and place of the proper relation of public and private goods.

We will not find an easy resolution of our problem in those theories. The problem of the relation of public and private goods, like the problem of the relation of the community to the individual, is one of the fundamental problems of political justice. It is the problem that philosophers and statesmen have grappled with for more than two millennia. But modern thinkers such as Thomas Hobbes and John Locke place the problem in stark relief, as an issue of political economy, and the contrasts (and similarities) between them help us see more precisely the difficulty we face.[1] Together, Hobbes and Locke can lead partisans of both sides to a better appreciation of the partiality of their positions and a better understanding of the claims on the other side. For all their differences, Hobbes and Locke recognize that there is no simple identity of public and private interests or rights.

Hobbes and Locke are often paired. Both are 17th-century English philosophers (though separated by a generation). Both are state-of-nature theorists who articulate teachings of natural equality and natural liberty, and both describe civil society and government as artifacts of human invention.

The two are also very often contrasted (and their differences regarding the origin of private property are among the most significant).[2] Yet what we often take to be their differences—the bumper sticker description of their differences—actually obscures their teachings and makes each less interesting than he really is. For example, both Hobbes and Locke give an account of a state of nature—a pre-political condition, perhaps meant anthropologically (an historical epoch in a long ago age), or perhaps a hypothetical condition (what human life would be like without government). Hobbes famously explains that in the state of nature there is no "mine and thine," and "no place for industry, because the fruit thereof is uncertain, and consequently, no culture of the earth . . . no commodious building . . . no knowledge of the face of the earth."[3] In Hobbes' account, the condition of perfect liberty and equality—our natural, ungoverned condition—is a state of war: a war of all against all that produces a condition that is "solitary, poor, nasty, brutish, and short."[4] On the other hand, Locke describes a state of nature that includes natural rights to property and therefore an account of natural justice. Locke carefully distinguishes the state of nature from the state of war and describes the state of nature initially as a state of "perfect freedom" and "equality," governed by a "law of nature" that teaches anyone "who will but consult it" that "no one ought to harm another."[5] In describing the "plain difference" between the state of nature and a state of war, Locke writes that they are "as far distant, as a State of Peace, Good Will, Mutual Assistance, and Preservation, and a State of Enmity, Malice, Violence, and Mutual Destruction are from one another."[6]

So Hobbes and Locke seem quite different in their accounts of our natural condition, and this leads them to address very different problems. Hobbes is concerned about our natural inclination toward chaos and war, and must explain how peace is produced. For Hobbes, the maintenance of public order is an absolute necessity and requires a nearly absolute sovereign. Locke, beginning more peaceably, must explain that his state of nature is subject to certain "inconveniences" that degenerate into war. But this means that Locke can conceive of a condition without politics that is, at least, livable. The maintenance of public order is, in Locke's language, a "convenience," and in his *Second Treatise* Locke uses the word "sovereignty" only twice.[7]

Hobbes and Locke therefore differ in their accounts of the politics that emerge out of this natural condition. To address the problem of the state of war—the state of natural confusion or chaos—Hobbes counsels that every state must claim, and be granted, absolute sovereign power, and indeed that we are simply fooling ourselves if we believe politics works in any other way. Anything less than acknowledging the absolute authority of the sovereign—say, if we were to declare allegiance to the sovereign in some cases but to God in others—can only breed dissent and ultimately civil war.[8] On the other hand, Locke famously argues that government must be founded on the consent of the governed, and that political power should be organized constitutionally into something like a system of separation of powers and checks and balances. Where Hobbes emphasizes the authority of the sovereign, Locke emphasizes the pre-eminence of a legislative power. Locke's two references to "sovereignty" in the *Second Treatise* are first as an example of a thing God has not granted to any person, and second to explain that only God is sovereign.[9]

And yet Hobbes' political account begins with a statement of natural liberty and natural equality—twin foundations of liberal politics—and Hobbes develops a prudential teaching of the importance of respecting the liberties of subjects. The Hobbesian subject retains something like a right to preserve himself—even if the threat to his preservation is the sovereign power itself. Hobbes understands that this right would be used to authorize the disorder he seeks to remedy. Therefore, he counsels that, though the sovereign has absolute power, prudence teaches the rule of law (and not mere monarchical will), establishment of a judicial appeals process, the exercise of a power to pardon, and security for legal property rights—all of which mitigate the danger of rebellion.[10]

Locke, who initially emphasizes natural equality and liberty and a government that is respectful of individual rights, eventually offers a teaching of extensive power. In his *An Essay Concerning Human Understanding* Locke gives two examples of moral propositions capable of scientific demonstration. The first is that *"Where there is no Property, there is no Injustice."* The second is that *"No government allows absolute Liberty"* (because the very *"Idea* of Government" is to govern "by certain Rules or Laws, which require Conformity").[11] In Locke's regime, too, we almost give up our natural right to preservation "to be regulated by Laws made by the society."[12] Locke was a political realist; in his hands, the principle of consent becomes "tacit and scarce avoidable," and expressed in practice by representatives of the majority rather than by independent individuals. The prerogative Locke describes for the executive is about as much as a Hobbesian could hope for, and bounded more by prudential considerations than by concerns of rights.[13] In Locke's own example it may be necessary to tear down "an innocent Man's House to stop the Fire, when the next to it is burning."[14] Locke understands, in agreement with Hobbes, that liberal politics works like any other regime to shape our habits of behavior and even our customs of thinking (though the particular habits and customs that liberalism inculcates may be different).

On investigation the similarity in the theoretical foundations of absolute and liberal governments seems disturbingly greater than their differences. When sovereign power understands the lessons of prudence, it moderates itself. And classical liberalism really does involve a quiet exercise of actual political power.

The Status of Property Rights

And yet there remains a further difference between the two philosophers that shapes their respective accounts of the state of nature, and
their political teachings as well. That difference is in their treatments
of the origin and extent of property rights. Hobbes insists that property is not natural, that it is rather a creation of the sovereign, subject to consent and political authority, and so readers should expect
extensive exercise of government authority over the private property
it has created. Locke insists that property rights are natural, held
even without the consent of others or of the political authority, and
so readers should expect an account of how those rights work to limit
the reach of government into private affairs. This difference carries
a most important implication: it is the origin and status of property
rights that marks the essential distinction between an authoritarian
political regime and a liberal one.[15]

Hobbes denies that property rights are natural. In the state
of nature there is no rule of "mine and thine," and no property.[16]
Indeed, in that original condition "every man has a right to everything, even to another's body."[17] As we might imagine, such a condition of disordered right "necessarily causeth war."[18] For Hobbes,
political authority is necessary for the very creation and security of
property; order precedes prosperity. Without a "coercive power"
to secure property under law, there can be no prosperity.[19] "[T]he
introduction of property," Hobbes writes, "is an effect of the commonwealth."[20] It is the sovereign who provides "nourishment" for
the principles of property, and the laws of mine and thine, and who
establishes rules of contract and exchange.[21] Thus we "erect a common power" to secure the fruits of our "industry."[22] It is therefore in
our interest to acquiesce in the establishment of political power.[23]

Though Hobbes refuses to provide a natural justice foundation for respect for private property rights, his prudential political
teaching aims to remedy the "poor" condition of our natural state
by establishing a law of private property. The economic policy that
follows is at once ordered by the sovereign authority to public ends,
and concerned to secure the benefits of private industry.[24] On the

one hand, the sovereign will assign land ownership in a way "agree-able to equity and the common good,"[25] and Hobbes reminds us that though these new, legal property rights will exclude intrusions and takings by other subjects, they do not exclude the authority of the sovereign.[26] Liberty, Hobbes reminds us, is not "an exemption from law."[27] Rather, it is the very purpose of civil law to abridge and restrain natural liberty.[28]

On the other hand, though the commonwealth itself may retain a portion of land, and order its cultivation and improvement (that is, the state may enter directly into economic activity), Hobbes advises against this.[29] Hobbes makes respect for property rights his sixth commandment of civil society.[30] Public ownership of the means of production runs the risk that one error costs everything; any monopolist will grow negligent. Moreover, such an expansive source of revenue threatens the unlimited expansion of government, and "Commonwealths can endure no diet."[31] In place of public ownership and management of the economy, Hobbes recommends the "equal imposition of taxes" to supply revenue for the defense of the commonwealth and for programs of public charity.[32] By "equal imposition" Hobbes means taxation proportional to "the debt that any man oweth to the commonwealth for his defence."[33] Because the wealthy receive an extra benefit from "the service of the poor" who work for them, Hobbes argues that the wealthy should contribute through their taxes for the defense and maintenance of the poor. Hobbes suggests that private charity is too unreliable, and too bound to private interests, to fulfill the public function of charity.[34] But he also insists that those recipients of charity who are physically capable must be required to work, perhaps by colonizing new lands.[35]

Hobbes' treatment of political economy moves in three stages. First, private property is an establishment of the sovereign, and therefore entirely subject to that sovereign authority. Second, Hobbes counsels that political prudence will lead the sovereign to restrain itself from too extensive an intervention in private economic life. Thus, third, Hobbes offers instead a system of proportional taxation and public charity.

In contrast, Locke insists that property rights are natural, and that each individual naturally holds a property right that is not at all dependent on the consent of others. In other words, we need no one's permission to build our own property, not even the permission of the government.[36] At the root of Locke's account is the natural ownership of each person in his or her very self, and the "first and strongest desire," which is the desire for "self-preservation." That desire is "the foundation of a right to the Creatures."[37] Locke conceives of the natural liberty of individuals as a property right in themselves. Indeed, Locke defines "property" as a right to life and liberty as well as estate, and he does so almost from the beginning of the *Second Treatise* to almost the very end.[38] That private realm of ownership is part of the definition of the human and essential to Locke's political foundation. Labor—even labor on oneself—generates conceptions of justice and rights.[39] As human beings labor, they generate rights in property—the property becomes private because the labor mixes "something" of the laborer into the product.[40] For Locke, these natural property rights establish a limit on the reach of political authority and broaden the claim of individuals to exercise their own private judgment.

Locke was proud of his theory of property, and the chapter has generated a rich assortment of commentaries.[41] Six times in the chapter Locke reminds us of our condition "in [or "at"] the beginning."[42] The entire Lockean history of commerce can be traced through the author's "beginnings."[43] "[I]n the beginning" all the land and its fruits were in common, but God and our wants commanded men to labor.[44] That labor generated private rights and possessions. "[A]t the beginning" there were very few people, so this appropriation by labor left enough and as good for others.[45] In some places, Locke writes, that may still be true, but the invention of money and the consent to its use introduced a right to larger possessions than one can use. The problem of spoilage is removed, and with money a person can generate more labor—through paying wages to others—than he can actually perform himself.[46] This invention builds prosperity and improves the condition of even the lowliest day laborer, who now may live above the level of a primitive king.[47]

(Locke suggests that when all the land has been appropriated it may be necessary to preserve a public "commons" by compact for use by those who have no land of their own.)[48] "[I]n the beginning" men didn't desire more than they needed, but gold changed that.[49] At one and the same time, people and land became more productive and also accumulated more wealth than was naturally necessary. "[A]t the beginning" Cain and Abel needed only a few acres, but the population grew and with it the need for political boundaries.[50] "[I]n the Beginning" labor gave a right to property, to appropriate what had been common, but as land became scarce peoples defined and defended their political boundaries. Within those boundaries they developed law and the regulation of private property, to settle the property rights which industry began.[51] Locke advises that the proper employment of labor and resources is now "the great art of government" and that a "godlike" prince will use "established laws of liberty" for the "protection and incouragement" of labor and industry.[52]

Though Locke's state of nature seemed characterized by law and good will, in truth "Person and Possessions" are "constantly exposed to the Invasion of others."[53] Without political society—the protection it offers and the currency it makes available—men would have no temptation to labor beyond their immediate needs. To do so would even be accounted foolish.[54] But then, Locke must believe with Hobbes that in the natural condition there will be no security for industry. It is the defense of property, broadly understood, that moves the state of nature into the state of war,[55] and in that state where there is no government to settle the matter "the state of war, *once begun, continues.*"[56] It is to avoid this state of war that we make government.[57] Indeed, Locke tells us that "Government has no other end but the preservation of Property" (that is, of life, liberty, and estate).[58] In Locke's account we actually need government after all to secure the fruits of our labor.

We need only consider Locke's treatment of the legislative power to realize that in practice the work of securing private property while advancing the public good will involve an inherent tension between the two. Fairly early, when Locke begins his account of government proper, he reminds us that the purpose of the political community is to preserve the liberty and property of individuals, and that the legislative power "is obliged to secure every ones Property."[59] Toward the end of the work Locke again reminds us of that principle and adds that when the legislative arbitrarily invades the property (in this instance the "Lives, Liberties, or Fortunes") of the people it dissolves its legitimate political authority.[60] Yet in between, in the details of Locke's constitution, we find a justification of a much more extensive political authority to take property. While Locke constrains the legislative power so that it "*cannot take* from any Man any part of his *Property* without his own consent,"[61] in short order we learn instead that no part of the subjects' property can be taken without "their own consent,"[62] and then that the property owner must give "his own Consent, *i.e., the* Consent of the Majority," or even of the representatives of the majority.[63]

The Dangers of Private Dominion

Explicit in the works of both thinkers is the recognition that private goods do not simply comport with public ones. Hobbes centers his concern on the problem of monopolies, which he calls a private disease that threatens the public good.[64] Locke turns his attention to the problem of economic dominion, the ways that the private power of wealth may be used to generate political dominion over life and liberty. Both thinkers seem to conceive of the realm of political economy—the encounter of private rights with public goods—as a scene of perpetual political contest.

For Hobbes we need government to make property possible, but Hobbes tells us that the "general inclination of all mankind [is] a perpetual and restless desire for power after power, that ceaseth only in death."[65] This desire for power has an economic as well as a military form.[66] Hobbes describes three natural causes of war: competition, diffidence, and vainglory. Even if competition is managed by securing the fruits of honest industry, and even if diffidence or fear is resolved by the establishment of a sovereign, the problem of vainglory or pride remains.[67] One example of this pride is overvaluing one's own worth, or believing that one's economic worth should be a foundation for political power.[68] Thus private interests routinely assert a claim to authority in the public realm.

The disease of private interest has public consequences. One "disease" of a commonwealth is the inability to raise sufficient revenue, a condition that arises "from the opinion that every subject hath a property in his lands and goods exclusive of the sovereign's right to use of the same."[69] This inclination to advance one's own private interests is made worse when the wealth of the community "is gathered together in too much abundance in one or a few private men, by monopolies or by farms of the public revenues."[70] Hobbes is concerned that the new industrial life will create centers of power independent of the sovereign, and will be able to act contrary to the public good. He warns that this is especially the case of monopolies. Monopolies aim at "the particular gain of every adventurer," they set prices in ways "ill for the people" and not for "a common benefit to the whole body," and they encourage disputation with the sovereign authority.[71] Hobbes fears that the notion of a natural and absolute private right to property—one that excludes the right of the sovereign—will tend to the dissolution of the commonwealth itself. "[I]f the right of the sovereign also be excluded, he cannot perform the office they have put him into."[72]

At the same time Hobbes does not merely abandon his subjects to the arbitrary and overbearing will of an absolute monarch. The subject retains a "true liberty," bound by the purposes for which the political community was first formed. Those purposes include peace and defense, including the defense of the fruits of industry.[73] Thus, subjects retain rights to defend themselves, to resist force and imprisonment.[74] What Hobbes must envision, then, for all his concern to establish political authority and order, is a dynamic political process that includes the sovereign's prudent recognition of the value of private property even as the sovereign asserts the essential importance of public benefits and public order.[75]

Locke's defense of property rights properly understood is arguably the very heart of his political teaching, yet like Hobbes, Locke recognizes the distance between private advantage and the "common good." For Locke, we need government to secure the property that is naturally ours. It is "the great art of government" to secure "honest industry" by "established laws of liberty."[76] Yet in his work on education Locke tells us that there are two paired desires that we observe in children (and therefore, he argues, we know that the same desires are in adults). One of these is the desire for liberty. The other related desire is for dominion. Locke says the desire for dominion is pursued in two ways. It is pursued first by having others submit to one's will, and second through "property and possession, pleasing themselves with the power which that seems to give."[77] In the *First Treatise* Locke argues that "*Private Dominion*" over property gives "no *Sovereignty*."[78] He adds that propriety of an estate is a fundamentally different undertaking than political rule. Estates are "for the benefit and sole Advantage of the Proprietor, so that he may even destroy the thing." Politics, on the other hand, is for the "Preservation" and "the good of the Governed."[79] We seem to face here two standards of judgment, the rights of individuals and the good of the community, and as political philosophers since Plato have recognized those two poles do not easily align.

What Locke foresees, therefore, is a dynamic and unresolved political contest among diverse interests or factions. The natural right of property is rooted in the individual's right of preservation;[80] the reason individuals enter into civil society is the preservation of their property.[81] But in Locke's account society, too, has a right to preserve itself, even a "Native and Original Right" to preserve itself.[82] Locke is well aware that "private Mens Cases," even when these men "have a right," will not always move "the Body of the People,"[83] and that "examples of particular Injustice, or Oppression" may not be felt by the majority.[84] Locke has described a political condition in which the insolence of rulers gives rise to the "Turbulency of private Men," and of factions. Sometimes those factions represent a defense of private rights against oppression; sometimes those factions represent the assertion of private interests over and above the public interest.[85] The political contest over these conflicting claims of public and private interests, as Locke conceives it, is never settled, and it can never be settled finally because both private and public interests have a legitimate claim of right.

Liberalism and Human Flourishing

Hobbes and Locke, founders of classical liberalism in the modern era, both offer teachings of a natural condition of liberty and equality. That natural condition proves untenable, and either is or quickly becomes a state of war as each person asserts his or her own interests, and especially those material interests related to the right of preservation. As a response to that natural state of war, so-called liberal government is asked to respect and secure private natural rights, and to moderate or regulate the assertion of those rights. That is, we demand liberty, and also a defense against the dominion of others. Property, broadly understood, grounds the rights of individuals to govern themselves, and those rights also help establish a limit on the claims of others or the authority of the government.

On the one hand, the defense of private property emerges as both principled and prudent. On the other, these foundational thinkers offer a realistic appraisal of the relation of private property to public goods. Helpfully, the pursuit of private fortune can produce goods for the community. Hobbes and Locke anticipate later thinkers in that respect. But they both counsel that we ought not to kid ourselves into believing in an easy harmony of public and private conceptions of the good. Rather, civil life is characterized as a dynamic contest of assertions of the good. Just as much as the public power will contribute to the security of the private, and private powers to the material good of the public, so also will each act perpetually to check and balance (or impede) the other.

It is not at all clear whether such a regime can provide a very rich account of human flourishing. One paradox of modern liberalism is that while it secures a realm of privacy within which individuals may pursue private conceptions of the good, it also seems to undermine claims for ultimate or absolute goods. In Hobbes, "good and evil" are names that signify our "appetites and aversions."[86] Similarly in his *Essay Concerning Human Understanding* Locke recasts "good" and "evil" as "pleasure" and "pain."[87] Alan Ryan notes Hobbes' break with the classical teleological view of human nature and flourishing. Ryan concludes that for Hobbes there is no summum bonum toward which human beings move, but rather a summum malum from which they move away.[88] It is the fear of death, rather than conception of a good, that motivates action. In a very famous passage in the *Essay Concerning Human Understanding* Locke remarks "that the Philosophers of old did in vain enquire, whether *Summum bonum* consisted in Riches, or bodily Delights, or Virtue, or Contemplation: And they might have as reasonably disputed, whether the best Relish were to be found in Apples, Plumbs, or Nuts." Some relishes "produce the greatest Pleasure" or "Happiness" for one "particular Palate," and other relishes for another.[89] Locke advises that this "may serve to shew us the Reason, why, though all Men's desires tend to Happiness, yet they are not moved by the same Object. Men may chuse different things, and yet all chuse right."[90]

In the only other reference to a summum bonum in the *Essay*, Locke elaborates on the idea of the good as a matter of taste, but now he revises his account. Locke concludes "that *Morality* is *the proper Science, and Business of Mankind in general*; (who are both concerned, and fitted to search out their *Summum Bonum*,) as several Arts, conversant about several parts of Nature, are the Lot and private Talent of particular Men, for the common use of humane Life, and their own particular Subsistence in this World."[91] Locke would nurture and protect "the private Talent of particular Men" who are pursuing their own particular subsistence in this world, and coincidentally provide the conveniences for humane life. This is not quite a description of a common good. Rather it suggests two goods, a private one and a public one, that may coincide. Given the diversity of goods, what may be the greatest good for one may not be for another; the greatest good for many may not be quite the same as the greatest good for the few.[92] We may speculate that, for Locke, individuals each have, or discover, or construct, the summum bonum in their lives. As Locke remarks in another context, perhaps there are only "Individuals . . . different from one another."[93]

Liberalism thus seems an instrumental political arrangement, one that makes possible the private pursuit of diverse good lives without imposing a particular telos on its citizens. An essential instrument of this liberty—and therefore of the opportunity for human flourishing—is protection of the rights of private property. Rights of private property can ensure a level of sustenance and even independence that is instrumentally necessary for any good life.[94]

Though life in the liberal regime thus promises neutrality with respect to conceptions of the good, in practice the new liberal regime cannot help imposing its own conception of the good or the tolerable on its subjects. Liberalism is "not mere proceduralism, nor is it neutral with respect to ways of life or virtues."[95] While the regime permits private pursuits of diverse goods, it also largely consigns those pursuits to the private sphere. The public realm still insists on particular characteristic actions. The free individual who can make his own way or chart her own course in the world must have certain capacities. Such a person must be independent and hardworking. Because of the liberal foundation in natural equality and natural liberty, such a person must respect the independence and hard work of others. And so liberalism insists on certain modern virtues, including industriousness and self-reliance, and toleration and civility. It rewards innovation and pragmatism more than tradition and philosophic speculation. Goods of the soul may be pursued freely in private. Lives devoted to faith or philosophy, to heroic virtue, or to pleasure must be moderated in the service of peace, preservation, and prosperity.

No regime is truly neutral with respect to the good life. The instruments of liberal life become the ends in themselves, and these new good lives may lack the lofty allure or ambition of the old. Modern liberalism secures a realm of privacy that makes some human flourishing possible, but that may not incline us toward teleological conceptions of the good. In its elevation of the instruments of the good life, liberalism may even close our minds to conceptions of ultimate goods. Without a teleological account of human flourishing the idea of the greatest good becomes, for the philosophers of modern liberty, nothing more than a matter of taste, and taste is so much a matter of private judgment that we find it increasingly difficult to consider ultimate goods—and the common good—seriously. Thus egalitarian liberalism has a tendency toward relativism. And yet liberalism properly understood is not neutral; it asserts its own particular claim to the good. Taking liberalism's particular claim seriously would be the first step toward a serious reappraisal of the alternatives—and especially of the claims of faith, philosophy, and heroic virtue.

Notes

1. Alan Ryan argues that Hobbes' political science resembles modern economics in a most essential way, as an "optimal strategy" for seeking one's interests. Alan Ryan, "Hobbes' Political Philosophy," in *The Cambridge Companion to Hobbes*, ed. Tom Sorell (Cambridge: Cambridge University Press, 1996), 213. Michael Zuckert concludes that Locke is "the first to define political economy as the central task of politics." Michael Zuckert, *Natural Rights and the New Republicanism* (Princeton: Princeton University Press, 1994), 272. Leo Strauss holds that Locke's doctrine of property is the "most characteristic part" of his political teaching. Leo Strauss, *Natural Right and History* (Chicago: University of Chicago Press, 1953), 234.

2. C. B. Macpherson, *The Political Theory of Possessive Individualism: Hobbes to Locke* (Oxford: Oxford University Press, 2011, 1962); John Dunn, *The Political Thought of John Locke: An Historical Account of the Argument of the Two Treatises of Government* (New York: Cambridge University Press, 1969), esp. 77–83; Ramon M. Lemos, *Hobbes and Locke: Power and Consent* (Athens, GA: University of Georgia Press, 1978); Wolfgang von Leyden, *Hobbes and Locke: The Politics of Freedom and Obligation* (New York: St. Martin's Press, 1982); Asaf Z. Sokolowsi, *Metaphysical Problems, Political Solutions: Self, State, and Nation in Hobbes and Locke* (Larham, MD: Lexington Books, 2011); Zuckert, *Natural Rights and the New Republicanism*; and Ross Harrison, *Hobbes, Locke, and Confusion's Masterpiece: An Examination of Seventeenth Century Political Philosophy* (Cambridge: University of Cambridge Press, 2003).

3. Thomas Hobbes, *Leviathan*, ed. Edwin Curley (Indianapolis: Hackett Publishing, 1994), 13.13. References are to chapter and section.

4. Ibid., 13.9.

5. *Second Treatise*, in John Locke, *Two Treatises of Government*, ed. Peter Laslett (Cambridge: University of Cambridge Press, 1960), 6. References are to section.

6. Ibid., 19.

7. Ibid., 4 and 6.

8. Ryan, "Hobbes' Political Philosophy," 219–20. Ryan maintains that Hobbes' state of war is characterized especially by a desire for peace in a condition of extreme uncertainty. In other words, the Hobbesian man is motivated by a good; he is not himself nasty, though his condition is.

9. Locke, *Second Treatise*, 4 and 6.

10. Hobbes, *Leviathan*, 21.17–19 and 30.23. See especially Ryan, "Hobbes' Political Philosophy," 231–12 and 237–41; David P. Gauthier, *The Logic of Leviathan* (Oxford: Clarendon Press, 1969), 138–32; and Perez Zagorin, *Hobbes and the Law of Nature* (Princeton: Princeton University Press, 2009), 82–83 and 95.

11. John Locke, *An Essay Concerning Human Understanding*, ed. Peter Nidditch (New York: Oxford University Press, 1975), 4.3.18. Hereafter cited as *Essay*. References are to book, chapter, and section.

12. Locke, *Second Treatise*, 129.

13. Peter Josephson, *The Great Art of Government* (Lawrence: University Press of Kansas, 2002): 231–43; and Martin Seliger, *The Liberal Politics of John Locke* (New York: Frederick A. Praeger, 1968), 346–60.

14. Locke, *Second Treatise*, 159.

15. Zuckert, *Natural Rights and the New Republicanism*, 275–78.

16. Hobbes, *Leviathan*, 13.13.

17. Ibid., 14.4.

18. Ibid., 18.10.

19. Ibid., 15.3 and 13.9.

20. Ibid., 24.5 and 15.3; and Macpherson, *The Political Theory of Possessive Individualism*, 62–68 and 95–97. For von Leyden the distinction between Hobbes and Locke regarding the origin of the right of property (whether, as in Hobbes, all property rights are generated by the sovereign; or whether, as in Locke, that right is natural and pre-political) is one of the fundamental differences between the two philosophers. Hobbes' account of the origin of property is one of the things "Locke wishes to guard against." Von Leyden, *Hobbes and Locke*, 137. See also Zagorin, *Hobbes and the Law of Nature*, 70.

21. Hobbes, *Leviathan*, 24.5 and 24.10.

22. Ibid., 17.13.

23. Ibid., 15.4–5 and 15.16. See also *De Cive*, in Thomas Hobbes, *Man and Citizen*, ed. Bernard Gert (Indianapolis: Hackett Publishing, 1991), 12.7 (where Hobbes suggests that the majority mistakenly believes that property

can only be taken from them with their consent and upon a demonstrated public need); and Hobbes, *Leviathan*, 18.6.

24. Gauthier, *The Logic of Leviathan*, 143; Howard Warrender, *The Political Philosophy of Thomas Hobbes: His Theory of Obligation* (Oxford: Clarendon Press, 1957), 182–225; and Ryan, "Hobbes' Political Philosophy," 235.

25. Hobbes, *Leviathan*, 24.6.

26. Ibid., 24.7.

27. Ibid., 21.6.

28. Ibid., 26.8.

29. Zagorin, *Hobbes and the Law of Nature*, 81.

30. Mary Dietz, "Hobbes' Subject as Citizen," in *Thomas Hobbes and Political Theory*, ed. Mary G. Dietz (Lawrence, KS: University Press of Kansas, 1990), 109–10.

31. Hobbes, *Leviathan*, 24.8.

32. Ibid., 30.17–18.

33. Ibid., 30.17.

34. Ibid., 30.18 and 22.22.

35. Ibid., 30.19; Ryan, "Hobbes' Political Philosophy," 235; and Dietz, 117–18, note 68.

36. Zuckert, *Natural Rights and the New Republicanism*, 258–59. Compare John Gough, *John Locke's Political Philosophy: Eight Studies* (Oxford: Clarendon Press, 1973), 64 and 73–92; and Seliger, *The Liberal Politics of John Locke*, 286–87 and 292. C. B. Macpherson indicts Locke as a modern oligarch who equated the acquisition of wealth with rationality, justified a political class structure, and promoted a regime in which only men "with 'estate'" can claim full membership and political authority, but Macpherson's reading is not sustained by the text. Macpherson, *The Political Theory of Possessive Individualism*, 221–252.

37. *First Treatise*, in Locke, *Two Treatises of Government*, 86–88. For thorough accounts of the foundations of Locke's right of self-preservation, see Strauss, *Natural Right and History*, 225 and 248; and Thomas Pangle, *The Spirit of Modern Republicanism* (Chicago: University of Chicago Press, 1988). In Hobbes' account in *De Cive* also the claim of natural right arises from an instinct for preservation. Hobbes compares this instinct to the impulse by which "a stone moves downward." Thus self-preservation is not "against the dictates of reason," and "that which is not contrary to right reason, that all

men account to be done justly, and with right." Hobbes, *De Cive*, 1.7. See also Zagorin, *Hobbes and the Law of Nature*, 75.

38. Locke, *Second Treatise*, 27 and 221.

39. Peter C. Myers, *Our Only Star and Compass: Locke and the Struggle for Political Rationality* (Lanham, MD: Rowman & Littlefield, 1998), 191–93.

40. Locke, *Second Treatise*, 27–28.

41. Prominent among these are Macpherson, *The Political Theory of Possessive Individualism*; Strauss, *Natural Right and History*, 234–48; James Tully, *A Discourse on Property: John Locke and His Adversaries* (Cambridge: Cambridge University Press, 1980); Michael Kramer, *John Locke and the Origins of Private Property: Philosophical Explanations of Individualism, Community, and Equality* (Cambridge: Cambridge University Press, 1997); and Gopal Sreenivasan, *The Limits of Lockean Rights in Property* (New York: Oxford University Press, 1995).

42. Locke, *Second Treatise*, 35–38, 45, and 49.

43. All these references to "in" or "at" the beginning therefore resonate with, and perhaps substitute for, the biblical account. Consider Nasser Behnegar, "Locke and the Sober Spirit of Capitalism," *Society* 49 (2012): 131–38.

44. Locke, *Second Treatise*, 35. Ultimately, Locke rewrites the biblical version; rather than a condition of plenty, it becomes a condition of scarcity. See also Zuckert, *Natural Rights and the New Republicanism*, 260–62; Alan Ryan, "Locke and the Dictatorship of the Bourgeoisie," in *Life, Liberty, and Property: Essays on Locke's Political Ideas*, ed. Gordon Schochet (Belmont, CA: Wadsworth, 1971), 86–106; and Ramon M. Lemos, "Locke's Theory of Property," *Interpretation: A Journal of Political Philosophy* 5, no. 2 (Winter 1975): 226–44.

45. Locke, *Second Treatise*, 36.

46. Zuckert, *Natural Rights and the New Republicanism*, 268; and Kristin Shrader-Frechette, "Locke and the Limits on Land Ownership," *Journal of the History of Ideas* 54, no. 2 (April 1993): 201–20, esp. 206–11 and 215. Limitations on the acquisition of property prior to the invention of money are well-described by Sreenivasan, *The Limits of Lockean Rights in Property*, 31–63. Locke's theory of value, which seems at first a labor theory, proves more nuanced. See especially Karen Iverson Vaughn, "The Economic Background to Locke's Two Treatises of Government," in *John Locke's Two*

Treatises: New Interpretations, ed. Edward J. Harpham (Lawrence, KS: University Press of Kansas, 1992), 132; and Patrick Kelly, "All Things Richly to Enjoy: Economics and Politics in Locke's *Two Treatises*," *Political Studies* 36, no. 2 (June 1988): 273–93. In *Locke, Sciences and Politics*, Steven Forde finds that "the primitive or underlying right of property is collective, and it must be modified or altered in some way to bring about private property." Steven Forde, *Locke, Sciences and Politics* (New York: Cambridge University Press, 2013), 151.

47. Locke, *Second Treatise* 36 and 41.

48. Ibid., 35; Tully, *A Discourse on Property*, 126–30; and Shrader-Frechette, "Locke and the Limits on Land Ownership," 215. Compare Sreenivasan, *The Limits of Lockean Rights in Property* 30–31 and 50–55.

49. Locke, *Second Treatise*, 37.

50. Ibid., 38.

51. Ibid., 45.

52. Ibid., 42.

53. Ibid., 123.

54. Ibid., 46 and 41.

55. Ibid., 18.

56. Ibid., 20.

57. Ibid., 21.

58. Ibid., 94 and 124.

59. Ibid., 131.

60. Ibid., 221–22.

61. Ibid., 138.

62. Ibid., 139.

63. Ibid., 140. Josephson, *The Great Art of Government*, 212–25; and Ross J. Corbett, *The Lockean Commonwealth* (Albany: State University of New York Press, 2009), 53–56.

64. Hobbes, *Leviathan*, 29.18.

65. Ibid., 11.2.

66. Ibid., 11.3.

67. Ibid., 6.39 and 27.13.

68. Deborah Baumgold, "Hobbes's Political Sensibility: The Menace of Political Ambition," in *Thomas Hobbes and Political Theory*, ed. Mary G. Dietz (Lawrence, KS: University Press of Kansas, 1990), 74–77. Compare

Macpherson, 67–68. Another, perhaps more serious, example is overvaluing one's own wisdom. Hobbes, *Leviathan*, 11.13.

69. Hobbes, *Leviathan*, 29.18.

70. Ibid., 29.19; and Ryan, "Hobbes' Political Philosophy," 232.

71. Hobbes, *Leviathan*, 22.18–20.

72. Ibid., 29.10.

73. Ibid., 21.10.

74. Ibid., 21.11, 14.8, 14.29, and 15.22.

75. Baumgold, "Hobbes's Political Sensibility," 75; and Ryan, "Hobbes' Political Philosophy," 232.

76. Locke, *Second Treatise*, 42

77. John Locke, *Some Thoughts Concerning Education and of the Conduct of the Understanding*, edited by Ruth W. Grant and Nathan Tarcov (Indianapolis: Hackett Publishing, 1996), 103–5. Myers argues that the desire for dominion in property actually moderates the desire for dominion over persons. Myers, *Our Only Star and Compass*, 194.

78. Locke, *First Treatise*, 43 and 87.

79. Ibid., 92.

80. Locke, *Second Treatise*, 25–27.

81. Ibid., 222.

82. Ibid., 220.

83. Ibid., 208.

84. Ibid., 230.

85. Ibid., 230 and 240.

86. Hobbes, *Leviathan*, 15.40.

87. Locke, *Essay*, 2.20.2.

88. Ryan, "Hobbes' Political Philosophy," 216–17.

89. Locke, *Essay*, 2.21.55. Compare Pangle, *The Spirit of Modern Republicanism*, 178. Compare Aristotle's *Ethics* 7.13.1153b28–31, 10.5.1175a30, and 10.5.1176a10. Aristotle advises that "no single nature and no single characteristic condition is, or is regarded, as the best" for every individual (7.13.1153b28–31), that different people find pleasure in different activities (10.5.1175a30–36), and that "[t]he same things give delight to some and pain to others" (10.5.1176a10–12). What is sweet to a man in a fever is not so to a healthy man. Aristotle is thus able to suggest the taste of the healthy man as a standard of goodness, while acknowledging the diversity

of human goods.

90. Locke, *Essay*, 2.21.55, see also 1.3.6.

91. Locke, *Essay*, 4.12.11. In the immediate sequel Locke's example is the discovery of kin kina, cr quinine, which, he says, does more good than hospital charity. Locke, *Essay*, 4.12.12.

92. This modern emphasis on pleasure, pain, and preservation may distort this picture somewhat. In Locke's hands, preservation is a necessary instrumental good; all other goods require it. Yet we may imagine some instances in which pursuit of preservation may impede some other good (for example, honor). In his recent work John Yolton finds in Locke's *Essay* a quiet concern for beauty, an exploration of human and divine happiness, and a teleological acccunt of the development of the person. John W. Yolton, *The Two Intellectual Worlds of John Locke: Man, Person, and Spirits in the Essay* (Ithaca, NY: Cornell University Press, 2004), pp. 60–61, 79–84, 90, 117, and 120–21.

93. Locke, *Essay*, 3.6.38 and 3.10.20.

94. Gauthier, *The Logic of Leviathan*, 144; and Lemos, "Locke's Theory of Property," 236.

95. Stephen G. Salkever, "'Lopp'd and Bound': How Liberal Theory Obscures the Goods of Liberal Practice," in *Liberalism and the Good*, ed. R. Bruce Douglass, Gerald M. Mara, and Henry S. Richardson (New York: Routledge, 1990), 174, but see 167–75 passim. See also William A. Galston, "Liberal Virtues," *American Political Science Review* 82, no. 4 (December 1988): 1277–90; Douglas A. Casson, *Liberating Judgment: Fanatics, Skeptics, and the Politics of Probable Judgment* (Princeton: Princeton University Press, 2011), 166–76; Peter Berkowitz, *Virtue and the Making of Modern Liberalism* (Princeton: Princeton University Press, 1999), 87; and Josephson, *The Great Art of Government*, 281.

Rousseau on Economic Liberty
and Human Flourishing

JOHN T. SCOTT
University of California, Davis

Jean-Jacques Rousseau (1712–78) is perhaps best known today as a theorist of democracy, indeed as the first major thinker in the Western philosophical tradition to argue that democracy is the only legitimate form of political association. According to Rousseau, only a state in which the people make laws for themselves as citizens can solve what he terms the "fundamental problem" of politics: "How to find a form of association that defends and protects the person and goods of each associate with all the common force, and by means of which each, uniting with all, nonetheless obeys only himself and remains as free as before."[1] Rousseau is centrally concerned with freedom, and almost all readers and interpreters—sympathetic or critical—focus on what he means by "freedom" and how the natural freedom of the individual can be reconciled with collective self-government in which the citizen who refuses to obey the law must be, in his notorious phrase, "forced to be free."[2] Less often noticed about Rousseau's formulation of the "fundamental problem" of politics, and about his political theory in general, is the central importance of property, or of the "goods" of each associate as he phrases it when articulating this "fundamental problem." The right to acquire property is part of the natural freedom of the individual, and the protection of this property is a purpose of the political association on par with the protection of liberty itself.

What, then, is the role of economic liberty in Rousseau's political thought?

In order to address this question, it is necessary to take a step back and first gain a general understanding of the aims of Rousseau's philosophy as a whole, including his political thought. The Citizen of Geneva offers an important answer in the very first lines of the work that made him famous, the *Discourse on the Sciences and the Arts* (1751), the prize essay he wrote for the Academy of Dijon on the question of whether the advancement of the sciences and arts seen in the age of Enlightenment had purified morals. "Here is one of the greatest and noblest questions ever debated," he begins the essay: "This discourse is not concerned with those metaphysical subtleties that have spread to all fields of literature and from which the announcements of academies are not always exempt. Rather, it is concerned with one of those truths that pertain to the happiness of the human race."[3] Happiness, or we might say human flourishing, is the central concern of Rousseau's thought. Schematically speaking, then, we can see his early philosophical works as diagnosing the problem of human flourishing and his later works, including the *Social Contract*, as offering possible remedies. Thus, in the *Discourse on the Sciences and the Arts* (1751) he argues that the advancement of the sciences and the arts, and more generally what we might term the "civilizing" process, has in fact led to less happiness and virtue, to stunted souls and false societies. He continues this theme even more emphatically in the *Discourse on the Origin and Foundations of Inequality Among Men* (1755) by telling the story of the development of human nature through history as a tale of general decline in terms of freedom and happiness, a story in which economic developments including the division of labor and the establishment of property play a central role. In his later works, in turn, he might be said to put forward various proposals for promoting human flourishing and freedom, whether through the pedagogical project of *Emile, or On Education* (1762), through his own retreat from society to attain something like the freedom of natural man as recounted in the *Reveries of the Solitary Walker* (1776–78), or through the political project of the *Social Contract* (1762) and his other political writings.

What, then, is human flourishing for Rousseau, and what threatens it? All too briefly, the answer to the first question is that human flourishing has two dimensions: unity of soul and the "size" of the soul, or its energy or expansive quality. Since the issue of the role of economic liberty in Rousseau's thought pertains largely to the second question, namely the ways in which the economic activities of the individual and society threaten human flourishing, let me briefly sketch Rousseau's view of human flourishing before turning to his concerns about the threat economic activities can pose to human happiness.

As for the first dimension, unity of the soul, numerous interpreters have in various ways noted the importance of psychic unity or wholeness for Rousseau's account of human happiness.[4] Alternatively, to put the issue negatively and thus anticipate the answer to the question of what threatens human flourishing, numerous interpreters have focused on dividedness of soul as a concern that runs throughout Rousseau's thought. His concern with psychic division as a threat to happiness and virtue first appears in his *Discourse on the Sciences and the Arts* in a subtle manner, with his remarks about how the sort of "civility" prized by modern societies in Europe is actually a form of falseness that pits how we appear to others against how we actually are, thus dividing us:

> Before art had fashioned our manners and taught our passions to speak a borrowed language, our morals were rustic but natural, and differences in conduct announced those of character at first glance. Human nature, at bottom, was not better. But men found their security in the ease of seeing through one another, and that advantage, of which we no longer sense the value, spared them many vices.[5]

Rousseau's concern with psychic unity and division is much more prominent in the *Discourse on Inequality*. In his portrait of natural man in the state of nature, Rousseau emphasizes the independence, and thus freedom in that sense, that comes from natural man's lack of dependence on anyone—whether psychological, physical, or otherwise. Contrasting natural man to "civil man," therefore, he speaks of "the advantage of constantly having all one's strength at one's disposal, of always being ready for any eventuality, and of always carrying oneself, so to speak, wholly with oneself."[6] Natural man is a "whole" unto himself. That said, to anticipate the second dimension of "size" of soul, it must be admitted that natural man is a limited animal whose soul is necessarily "small," even if it has the advantage of being unified. Contrary to the common notion that Rousseau praises such a "noble savage" (for in fact he never uses this phrase), natural man is not a model for human beings or human happiness beyond the merely formal sense in that his soul is unified.

As humans emerge from the state of nature and form societies, however, the psychic unity tied to independence is lost due to the emergence of personal dependence. As humans develop, they come to have various forms of sustained interactions with one another, and these interactions ultimately lead to psychic and social divisions. In Rousseau's account this process happens very gradually, over the course of multitudes of centuries. At the point where human nature has, he states, reached nearly the stage of development of which it is capable, the corrupt fruits of this development become fully manifest. "For one's advantage, it was necessary to appear to be different from what one in fact was. To be and to appear to be became two entirely different things, and from this distinction came ostentatious display, deceitful cunning, and all the vice that follow in their wake."[7]

Contrary to Marx, for example, the psychological effects of dependence are not secondary or epiphenomenal to the underlying explanatory variable of the means of production, but economic concerns are nonetheless important aspects of Rousseau's account. The term Rousseau uses for what I have termed "interactions" above in speaking of how humans come to have sustained interactions with one another in Rousseau's account is "*commerce*" in French.[8] This terminology is revealing in two ways. First, since the term can mean "interactions" in general or commercial relations in particular, in Rousseau's account commercial or economic relations are a particular extension of human interactions in general, and so the threats to human flourishing associated with economic relations are part and parcel of a more general problem related to personal dependence and interdependence. Second, his use of the term and his diagnosis of the problems associated with "*commerce*" in either the broad or specific sense put him into dialogue with other thinkers of his time who argue for the beneficial effects of "*commerce*," as we shall see below.

As for the role of "*commerce*" in the narrower sense of economic relations in Rousseau's account of our loss of psychic unity, its effects are seen even prior to the establishment of property in the form of proto-property and a primitive division of labor. For example, with what he terms "the epoch of a first revolution" occurring with the establishment and differentiation of families, Rousseau writes that "a sort of property" was introduced, both in the form of huts and other lodgings and in the form of family members themselves ("my" wife). Likewise, this revolutionary development led to a primitive division of labor and the consequent increase in production, though not a happy development in Rousseau's telling:

> And this was the first yoke they imposed on themselves without thinking about it and the first source of the evils they prepared for their descendants. . . . Since [these new needs] had degenerated into true needs, being deprived of them became much more cruel than their possession was sweet, and they were unhappy to lose them without being happy to possess them.[9]

But the eventual establishment of property with the dual discovery of agriculture and metallurgy is the decisive moment in Rousseau's story. Notably, the statement quoted just above about the internal division we experience between the requirements of being and appearing occurs within his discussion of the establishment of property. Since natural talents are unequal, he argues, property is bound to become unequal, and this inequality becomes institutionalized and no longer tied to natural inequalities when property becomes a social or political convention and is transferable and heritable. With rich and poor comes dependence on each side, and thus both psychological and economic dependence. The passage quoted just above concerning the gap between being and appearing therefore continues with Rousseau looking at the new situation from a different angle: "From another point of view, having previously been free and independent, here is man, subjected, so to speak, by a multitude of new needs to all of nature and especially to his fellow humans, whose slave he in a sense becomes even in becoming their master."[10]

The establishment of property is the key turning point in Rousseau's account of human history and the psychic costs it exacts. He signals the critical importance of this development at the outset of the Second Part of his *Discourse*:

> The first person who, having enclosed a plot of ground, thought of saying "this is mine" and found people simple enough to believe him was the true founder of civil society. What crimes, wars, murders, what miseries and horrors, would the human race have been spared by someone who, pulling up the stakes or filling in the ditch, had cried out to his fellow humans: "Beware of listening to this imposter. You are lost if you forget that the fruits are everyone's and the earth is no one's!"[11]

Nonetheless, Rousseau pours some cold water on this hot rhetoric by continuing: "in all likelihood things had already reached a point where they could no longer remain as they were."[12] Rather than advocate the abolition of private property, for example, Rousseau will accept property, the division of labor, and commerce, but all with a view to their costs in terms of psychic unity and therefore human flourishing.

The second dimension of human flourishing is the "size" of soul, or its energy or expansiveness, a dimension that has received far less attention from interpreters than the first dimension of unity.[13] The connection between these two dimensions can be glimpsed in the beginning of Rousseau's educational treatise, *Emile*. Rousseau explains there that, given the contradictions between nature and social institutions in terms of human psychology, "one must choose between making a man or a citizen, for one cannot make both at the same time." Both "man" and "citizen" possess psychic unity, but psychic unity of very different kinds:

> Natural man is entirely for himself. He is numerical unity, the absolute whole which is relative only to itself or its kind. Civil man is only

a fractional unity dependent on the denominator; his value is determined by his relation to the whole, which is the social body. Good social institutions are those that best know how to denature man, to take his absolute existence from him in order to give him a relative one and transport the *I* into the common unity, with the result that each individual believes himself no longer one but a part of the unity and no longer feels except within the whole.[14]

This passage in *Emile* should be compared to what Rousseau writes in the *Social Contract* about the task of the "Lawgiver": "He who dares to undertake to establish a people's institutions must feel that he is capable of changing, so to speak, human nature; of transforming each individual, who by himself is a complete and solitary whole, into a part of a greater whole from which that individual receives as it were his life and his being."[15] How freedom is consistent with such denaturing or being "forced to be free" is, of course, an important issue, and Rousseau might even be said to value psychic unity over freedom.

To return to the opening of *Emile*, Rousseau's concern is that trying to make an individual simultaneously good for himself (a "man") and good for others (a "citizen") leads to psychic disunity as well as a "smaller" or weaker soul, in large part because it is divided.

He who in the civil order wants to preserve the primacy of the sentiments of nature does not know what he wants. Always in contradiction with himself, always floating between his inclinations and his duties, he will never be either man or citizen. He will be good neither for himself nor for others. He will be one of these men of our days: a Frenchman, an Englishman, a bourgeois. He will be nothing.[16]

The psychic disunity Rousseau describes also makes this neither-man-nor-citizen small-souled. The contradiction he experiences within himself absorbs the strength of the soul, making him "smaller," even "nothing." Later in the same work, Rousseau diagnoses what makes us unhappy is "the disproportion between our desires and our faculties. A being endowed with senses whose faculties equaled his desires would be an absolutely happy being." In such a condition, we "enjoy our whole being," he says.[17] Rousseau's conception of the second dimension of the "size" of the soul when superadded to the first dimension of psychic unity can thus be seen as an actualization of our nature, and thus to some extent similar to what Aristotle means by human flourishing, or *eudaimonia*, though on a very different understanding of human nature. In sum, Rousseau's project, or rather projects, in making a "man" (*Emile*, perhaps the *Reveries*) or making a "citizen" (*Social Contract*) can therefore be seen as attempting to maximize the two dimensions of psychic unity and "size" of soul that provide the necessary conditions for human flourishing.

Rousseau's use of the term "bourgeois" to denote the small-souled product of modern society—arguably the first recorded usage of the term in the sense in which we now understand it—provides a convenient opportunity to turn to the relationship between economics and human flourishing in his thought by way of contrasting his position on these issues to that of his contemporaries. As noted above, Rousseau uses the term "*commerce*" in the broad sense of human interactions and the narrow sense of economic relations, and in doing so he enters into a debate with his contemporaries over the effects of "*commerce*" in both senses.[18] A number of prominent thinkers, mostly in what we would term the tradition of liberal political thought and including Montesquieu, Hume, and Smith, among others, argued that "*commerce*" had positive effects on the manners and mores of peoples. Among other things, they argued that "*commerce*" "softened" morals and manners, hence what is known as the theory of "*doux commerce*."[19] In arguing for such "*commerce*" these liberal thinkers were contesting classical republican theories that tended rather to emphasize "harder" or more martial virtues and to see commercial relations as threatening to those virtues.

Rousseau taps into this republican tradition in condemning the "softening" effects of modern commercial societies. This condemnation is particularly evident in the *Discourse on the Sciences and the Arts* with his laments over the loss of martial virtues in modern societies.[20] Although he draws on such republican rhetoric, Rousseau's own concern with the effects of "*commerce*" is nonetheless based on his particular conception of human nature and human flourishing. His more general case against his opponents in liberal tradition can be seen in a defense of the *Discourse on the Sciences and the Arts* in what he calls the "most arresting and most cruel" truth he has put forward there:

> All our writers regard the crowning achievement of our century's politics to be the sciences, the arts, luxury, commerce, laws, and all the other bonds which, by tightening the social ties among men through self-interest, place them all in a position of mutual dependence, impose on them mutual needs and common interest, and oblige everyone to contribute to everyone else's happiness in order to secure his own. These are certainly fine ideas, and they are presented in an attractive light. But when they are examined carefully and impartially, the advantages which they seem at first to hold out prove to be subject to a good many reservations. [21]

Having made this pronouncement, Rousseau turns to his familiar laments over the division between being and appearance this mutual dependence creates and their corrupting effects on virtue and happiness.[22] If Rousseau follows progenitors of the theory of "*doux commerce*" such as Hobbes and Locke, as well as these liberal thinkers themselves, by arguing that humans are driven first and foremost by self-love or self-interest, he is much less sanguine than they are about relying on unrestrained, or even somewhat restrained, self-interest. For Rousseau, self-interest or self-love is simply too strong and likely to degenerate into corrupt forms of pride, vanity, and petty self-interest. Combined with the deleterious effects of mutual dependence, this corrupted form of self-love is a toxic recipe for human flourishing.

Having discussed Rousseau's conception of human flourishing and the threat to it posed by the process of socialization in general and by modern commercial societies in particular, we can now turn to his thoughts on the role of economic liberty in his political thought and how the economic realm, including economic liberty, might be arranged to minimize the threat it poses.

We have already seen at the outset that Rousseau makes property, or the "goods" of each associate, along with liberty itself, central to the "the fundamental problem" of politics as he frames it in the *Social Contract*. Somewhat later in the same work, in the often neglected chapter "On Real Property" (Book I, Chapter 9), Rousseau explains that by entering into the social compact the "possessions" of each associate become "property" fully speaking. Following Locke, Rousseau argues that property begins through possession by what he terms in this context "private individuals,"[23] and elsewhere he presents an even more Lockean theory of property by arguing that it originates by the admixture of labor and is justified by that fact.[24] Yet he argues that property "becomes a true right only after the right of property has been established," and that this only happens with the institution of the social contract. Within the political association, then, it is the sovereign that determines "mine" and "thine," and so there is no absolute individual right to property for Rousseau (and nor is there for Locke either, contrary to what is usually thought). While many readers might see this sovereign authority over property as a threat to individual liberty and well-being, Rousseau emphasizes the gain in the transaction: "What is extraordinary about this alienation [of property] is that the community, far from despoiling private individuals of their goods by accepting them, merely assures them of their legitimate possession and transforms usurpation into a genuine right and use into property."[25]

The importance of property in Rousseau's conception of the purpose of the social contract is more prominent in a lesser-known work predating the *Social Contract* by a few years, his essay "On Political Economy" ("*Economie politique*") first published in 1755 as an article in the *Encyclopédie* edited by Diderot and d'Alembert. Those who turn to the essay "On Political Economy" to learn about Rousseau's views on political economy—or economics generally—as they are usually conceived will be largely disappointed, for Rousseau's article focuses mainly on the formation of citizen virtue to ensure the smooth running of the state. This is a perfectly legitimate way in which to understand the "economy" of politics given the sense of the word "economy" during this period as meaning the operation of a complex system, such as the "economy of the solar system" or "economy of nature." (Nonetheless, apparently the editors of the *Encyclopédie* were dissatisfied with Rousseau's effort and therefore took advantage of the alternate spelling of the word, etymologically derived from the Greek *oikos*, and commissioned another article under the title "*Oeconomie politique*.") Although Rousseau only turns to the subject of the economic policies of the state at the end of his article, almost as an afterthought, property nonetheless is central to the political theory he outlines in the work.

Rousseau begins the essay "On Political Economy" by establishing some basic principles about the legitimate state, and in fact this essay is the occasion for his first use of the term "general will," although his elaboration of the concept will have to await the *Social Contract*. His focus in the essay is on how the institution of law solves what he will call the "fundamental problem" of politics in his later political treatise. He writes: "By what inconceivable art could the means have been found to subjugate men in order to make them free; to use the goods, the labor, even the life of its members in the service of the state without forcing and without consulting them; to bind their will with their own consent. . . . These marvels are the work of the law."[26] The rule of law, then, is the source of freedom within political societies.

But once again, according to Rousseau, humans are naturally self-interested and also short-sighted in pursuing their self-interest; they do not see that obeying the law is the source of their freedom, or they believe they can enjoy the benefits of the state without shouldering its burdens. Given the incongruity of human nature and the necessities of citizenship, therefore, Rousseau gives most of his attention in the essay to how citizens must be educated in such a way to learn to love their fatherland and thereby to learn to identify their own self-interest with the common interest. "Do you want the general will to be fulfilled? Make sure that all private wills are related to it; and since virtue is only this conformity of the private will to the general, to say the same thing briefly, make virtue reign."[27] Rousseau therefore turns to a lengthy discussion of civic education associated more with ancient political theory and practice, such as Plato's *Republic* or Spartan and Roman practices. This focus is not unique to this early essay, for the longest chapter of the *Social Contract* (Book IV, Chapter 8) is on the subject of civil religion, and Rousseau likewise appeals to civic education in his late *Considerations on the Government of Poland* (1772). The primacy of *politics* and political liberty over *economics* and economic liberty in Rousseau's thought is clear here as elsewhere.

Nonetheless, the reader of "On Political Economy" who is accustomed to the view of Rousseau as a proponent of the "liberty of the ancients" over the "liberty of the moderns," to use Constant's terms, is in for something of a surprise. When he finally turns in the essay to matters of political economy in the ordinary sense, he introduces the subject with a seemingly very un-Rousseauan statement: "It is certain that the right of property is the most sacred of all the rights of citizens, and more important in certain respects than freedom itself," and he argues that "property is the true basis of civil society and the true guarantee of the citizens' engagements." What exactly Rousseau means here is not entirely clear, but he seems to be arguing that property is the "true basis" of society because the protection of their goods is perhaps even the primary reason the parties to the social contract agree to form the state and that property is the "true guarantee" of the citizens' engagements because it makes them "answerable" to the law, as he phrases it, in a way that not having property to protect would not.[28] Part of this responsibility rooted in the protection of property furthermore obliges the citizens to use their property to support the expenses incurred in the administration of the state through taxation.

Whatever the "sanctity" of the right of property and its role as the "true basis" of civil society, for Rousseau economics must be subordinated to the overarching goals of politics. Rousseau's emphasis in "On Political Economy," as in the *Social Contract* and elsewhere, is therefore less on economic liberty than on the regulation of economics and property. In this light, then, equality is as important in Rousseau's conception of a proper system of legislation as freedom. In the *Social Contract* he therefore writes:

> If one investigates in what precisely consists the greatest good of all—
> which should be the end of every system of legislation—one will find

that it comes down to the following two principal objects: *freedom*
and *equality*. Freedom, because any particular dependence is that
much force taken away from the body of the state. Equality, because
freedom cannot endure without it.[29]

As for freedom, note Rousseau's concern with the problem of personal dependence, which we saw above was the primary threat to
human flourishing through the way in which it divides and ener-
vates the soul. As for equality, Rousseau explains that the citizens
need not be absolutely equal, including in terms of property, but
he does argue that there should be limitations to inequality: "with
regard to wealth, no citizen should be so extremely rich that he can
buy another and none so poor that he is constrained to sell himself."[30] If we recall his discussion in the *Discourse on Inequality* of
the establishment of property and the psychic and social effects it
has due to the mutual dependence of the rich and the poor, we can
understand the thrust of Rousseau's concern here.

While Rousseau recognizes that individuals—and the state—
must eat, and therefore offers proposals to foster economic development, largely in the realm of agriculture, his vision is rather Spartan,
so to speak. As opposed to his contemporaries in the tradition
of "*doux commerce*," who see the creation and satisfaction of new
needs as an engine of economic growth and prosperity, among other
things, Rousseau views these novel necessities as dangerous, as we
have already seen in his discussion in the *Discourse on Inequality* of
the superfluities made possible by the primitive division of labor. In
"On Political Economy" he writes: "If one examines how the needs
of a state grow, this will often be found to happen in about the same
way as it does for private individuals, less by true necessity than by
an expansion of frivolous desires, and often expenses are increased
solely to provide a pretext for increasing revenue."[31] He therefore
concludes that the "most important maxim of the administration of
finances is to work much more carefully to prevent needs than to
increase revenues."[32] As for taxation, Rousseau agrees with Locke
that the state only has the right to tax its citizens with their consent.
However, in addition to trying to prevent the economic conditions

that produce inequality in the first place, Rousseau advocates "equitable and truly proportional" taxation that has the effect of decreasing inequality.[33]

In conclusion, then, for Rousseau economics and economic liberty are in the service of politics and political liberty, as he conceives of it, and he assesses both the possibilities and dangers of both politics and economics from the vantage point of his understanding of the requirements of human flourishing. Earlier, when discussing his conception of human flourishing, I noted that his desire to realize the two dimensions of which human flourishing is comprised, psychic unity and "size" of soul, could be compared to Aristotle's *eudaimonia*. Nonetheless, there is a critical difference between their understandings of human nature: for Rousseau humans are not the "political animal" of Aristotle and, in fact, are naturally asocial. Natural asociality is in fact what enables Rousseau's natural man to exist without any form of dependence on his fellow humans and is thus the basis for his psychic unity or wholeness. Any form of social connection is, at least in principle, contrary to human nature for Rousseau, and thus poses a threat to human flourishing or at least needs to be carefully managed to limit that threat. Economic activity and economic liberty are one such form of social connection, and Rousseau's counsel to impose limits on this activity and liberty stems from his concern with the delicate and urgent matter of human happiness.

Notes

1. Jean-Jacques Rousseau, *On the Social Contract*, Book I, chap. 6, in *The Major Political Writings of Jean-Jacques Rousseau*, trans. and ed. John T. Scott (Chicago: University of Chicago Press, 2012), 172.

2. Rousseau, *Social Contract*, I.7.175.

3. Jean-Jacques Rousseau, *Discourse on the Sciences and the Arts*, in *The Major Political Writings of Jean-Jacques Rousseau*, 7.

4. See, for example, Arthur M. Melzer, *The Natural Goodness of Man: On the System of Rousseau's Thought* (Chicago: University of Chicago Press, 1990); and John T. Scott, "The Theodicy of the *Second Discourse*: The 'Pure State of Nature' and Rousseau's Political Thought," *American Political Science*

Review 86 (September 1992): 696–711.

5. Rousseau, *Discourse on the Sciences and the Arts*, 13.

6. Jean-Jacques Rousseau, *Discourse on Inequality*, in *The Major Political Writings of Jean-Jacques Rousseau*, 67.

7. Ibid., 100.

8. For Rousseau's uses of the term *"commerce"* in this context, see ibid., 93, 95, 97, and 103.

9. Ibid., 94–95.

10. Ibid., 100.

11. Ibid., 91.

12. Ibid.

13. Lawrence D. Cooper is largely responsible for revealing the importance of this second dimension of the expansive character of the soul for Rousseau's conception of human nature and happiness. See Lawrence D. Cooper, *Rousseau, Nature, and the Problem of the Good Life* (University Park, PA: Pennsylvania State University Press, 1999).

14. Jean-Jacques Rousseau, *Emile, or On Education*, trans. and ed. Allan Bloom (New York: Basic Books, 1979), 39–40.

15. Rousseau, *Social Contract*, II.7.191.

16. Rousseau, *Emile*, 40.

17. Ibid., 80.

18. See Dennis C. Rasmussen, *The Problems and Promise of Commercial Society: Adam Smith's Response to Rousseau* (University Park, PA: Pennsylvania State University Press, 2008), chap. 1.

19. See Albert O. Hirschman, *The Passions and the Interests: Political Arguments for Capitalism Before Its Triumph* (Princeton, NJ: Princeton University Press, 1977).

20. Rousseau, *Discourse on the Sciences and the Arts*, 28–30.

21. Jean-Jacques Rousseau, *Preface to "Narcissus,"* in *The Discourses and Other Early Political Writings*, trans. and ed. Victor Gourevitch (Cambridge, UK: Cambridge University Press, 1997), 100–101.

22. Ibid.

23. Rousseau, *Social Contract*, I.9.176.

24. Rousseau, *Emile*, 97–99.

25. Rousseau, *Social Contract*, I.9.177.

26. Jean-Jacques Rousseau, "On Political Economy," in *On the Social*

Contract, with Geneva Manuscript and Political Economy, trans. Judith R. Masters, ed. Roger D. Masters (New York: St. Martin's, 1978), 214.

27. Rousseau, "On Political Economy," 217.

28. Ibid., 224–25.

29. Ibid.

30. Rousseau, *Social Contract*, II.11.200.

31. Rousseau, "On Political Economy," 228.

32. Ibid., 227.

33. Ibid., 230.

Adam Smith and Human Flourishing

RYAN PATRICK HANLEY
Marquette University

It is difficult to imagine two things more different, on their face, than public policy and political philosophy. One is concrete; the other abstract. One provides solutions; the other asks questions. One responds to the challenges of the moment; the other to challenges that have been with us from the earliest times.

Yet for all these differences, the divorce of political philosophy from public policy would be fatal to each. The policymaker who limits his vision to what can be done and is deaf to questions about what ought to be done seems as dangerous as the philosopher who focuses on the ideal and ignores the real conditions of human beings. Bringing the two enterprises together thus seems necessary for the success of each individually. It is especially necessary when the substantive issue at stake concerns the relationship of human flourishing to economic liberty—a relationship that was particularly well understood by Adam Smith, one of the modern world's most careful and insightful students of both public policy and political philosophy.

Adam Smith is of course today famous for his defense of economic liberty and thus as a founding father of capitalism. In his book *The Wealth of Nations*, Smith laid out a comprehensive defense of what he called "commercial society," analyzing at length and in detail the policies of a market society and their several advantages over more restrictive policies associated with alternative forms of economic order. The book is today remembered largely for its images and metaphors: the pin factory that shows the remarkable advantages of divided, specialized labor and the invisible hand that generates wealth and promotes its distribution. Yet those who have read the whole book know that its primary focus is public policy—evident in the simple fact that *The Wealth of Nations* invokes the invisible hand only once, but cites and studies no less than 266 discrete English statutes and Scottish parliamentary acts.

Smith's credentials as both a champion of economic liberty and a policy wonk are thus solid. But his interests hardly end here and in fact extend to the concept of human flourishing. In what follows, I argue that Smith's credentials on this philosophical front are every bit as solid as those on the practical economic front. In particular I argue that Smith thought long and hard about the concept of human flourishing and, most importantly, that the vision of human flourishing he developed is itself the grounds for his defense of economic liberty.

If this is right, it has implications for how we understand Smith and for how we understand the relationship of philosophy to policy. On the first front, the main implication of the view I want to defend is that Smith's defense of the superiority of market orders rests not on concerns with simple utility maximization, but rather on the belief that markets are indispensable to human flourishing. Put in this volume's terms, Smith's defense of the economic liberty fundamental to capitalism is founded on the belief that economic liberty is not an end in itself, but a means to the greater end of promoting the flourishing of both individuals and societies. And on the latter front, the main claim I want to defend is that Smith, insofar as he brings together the concerns of both policy and philosophy, remains a useful model for those of today's legislators seeking to transcend mere ideology and instead articulate a vision for an enlightened public policy informed by political philosophy.

Economic Flourishing

A comprehensive survey of Smith's moral and political philosophy lies well beyond the limited space available here.[1] What follows focuses on three discrete claims that Smith advances in three separate passages. Each passage focuses on the concept of human flourishing, and analyzed and read in context, they illuminate not only Smith's understanding of human flourishing but also the foundations of his defense of economic liberty. Yet the three passages, while all focused on human flourishing, treat different sides of the concept, with one focused on what we might call economic flourishing, the second on political flourishing, and the third on moral flourishing.

We begin with the first of these: economic flourishing. Smith uses the term "flourishing" in a variety of places in *The Wealth of Nations*, often in the context of describing the flourishing condition of a particular trade or particular manufacture in a particular country.[2] So far as I know, only once in the text does he invoke the explicit concept of flourishing in its traditional, philosophical sense of referring to the healthy state of a society or individual. But it is a very important reference, one that well deserves the attention of both Smith specialists and students of capitalism more generally.

The reference comes in the midst of Smith's chapter on the wages of labor in the first book of *The Wealth of Nations*. Its specific context is Smith's intervention in a current debate over the relative desirability of "improvement in the circumstances of the lower ranks of the people."[3]

Not everyone welcomed the prospect of improvement in the condition of the poor. Smith was intimately familiar with the counterargument that higher wages for laborers would translate into a new taste for luxury, leading to dissatisfaction with previous conditions, as well as the claim that high wages would tend to sap industriousness and incentivize laziness. But Smith rejected such claims on the grounds of human flourishing:

> Is this improvement in the circumstances of the lower ranks of the people to be regarded as an advantage or as an inconveniency to the society? The answer seems at first sight to be abundantly plain. Servants, laborers and workmen of different kinds, make up the far greater part of every great political society. But what improves the circumstances of the greater part can never be regarded as an inconveniency to the whole. No society can surely be flourishing and happy, of which the far greater part of the members are poor and miserable. It is but equity, besides, that they who feed, clothe, and lodge the whole body of the people, should have such a share of the produce of their own labor as to be themselves tolerably well fed, clothed, and lodged.[4]

This is a striking and important passage for several reasons. Some of these concern what they reveal about Smith, while others concern their implications for how best to understand market orders and their benefits today.

On the former front, the passage especially clarifies the degree to which Smith cannot be reduced to a caricature view that defines the good society as that in which the most talented few enjoy the maximum possible opportunities for achievement and self-advancement. Smith of course values the utility of the free pursuit of self-interest. But freedom to pursue self-interest alone neither defines a flourishing society nor justifies a market order. As made clear here, what defines the flourishing society is not the condition of the few but the condition of the majority; indeed, only when the "far greater part" of a society no longer lives in a state of indigence can the society be said to flourish.

The measure of the good society is thus at least as much the state of the worst-off as that of the well-off. And as Smith here and elsewhere explains, the proper measure of this state is whether the worst-off are able to acquire goods relatively easily. In his university lectures on jurisprudence, Smith defined this state of flourishing via the concept of "comeattibleness"—that is, the relative ease by which even the most indigent can "come at," or acquire via purchase, goods.[5]

Smith dropped this awkward phrase when he revised his thoughts for *The Wealth of Nations*. Yet the concept remains central to his published defense of market orders. In short, his argument is that the market is desirable not as an end in itself, or merely because it makes possible economic growth, but because it alleviates the condition of the poor and thereby helps to realize the flourishing society. This is the departure point for *The Wealth of Nations* itself, as made clear in its opening chapter, which argues that the superiority of the well-governed society consists precisely in its capacity to achieve "that universal opulence which extends itself to the lowest ranks of the people" and thereby ensure that "a general plenty diffuses itself through all the different ranks of the society."[6]

Now, this view of Smith may surprise some. Within the Beltway, Smith tends to be regarded as the property of the Republicans whose ties bear his portrait rather than bleeding hearts. But recent scholars have reopened debate on this front, asking the question—to borrow the title of an important recent article—"Adam Smith: Left or Right?"[7] The question has seen a number of prominent academic voices weigh in on either side. But perhaps the most important effect of this debate is to help us see the degree to which Smith—and especially his conception of human flourishing—transcends narrowly partisan concerns.

An anecdote may help show this. I spent the afternoon prior to delivering the first version of these remarks playing tourist and going for a walk around the Tidal Basin. My destination was the Jefferson Memorial. I had visited it several times prior, having grown up not far from Washington, DC. But I had never before visited the Franklin Delano Roosevelt Memorial. Visiting it that day, perhaps because I was thinking of Smith, I was struck by the quotation from FDR's second inaugural address that dominates the memorial's "room" dedicated to the New Deal years: "The test of our progress is not whether we add more to the abundance of those who have much; it is whether we provide enough for those who have too little."

Is FDR then a faithful follower of Adam Smith? Clearly not, in one key sense; his casting of the question as one of how "we" ought to "provide" for the poor points toward a role for political agency that much in Smith's system resists.

Yet even if Smith and FDR stand on opposite sides of the fence on the question concerning who ought to provide for the poor and how such relief is best provided, they agree that the flourishing of a society is measured by the conditions of the poor. For all their disagreements on means, FDR and Smith envision the same ends, and together they point to a view of human flourishing that transcends familiar partisan distinctions.

Political Flourishing

Attending to Smith's passage on flourishing in *The Wealth of Nations* helps clarify not only his conception of human flourishing itself but also the way in which he understood the relationship of human flourishing to economic liberty. In particular, it helps us see that Smith defined the flourishing economic order not as that which allows only a part of society to benefit, but one that instead promotes the flourishing of society as a whole. Smith's second key passage on flourishing points in a similar direction. This second passage is to be found not in *The Wealth of Nations*, but in *The Theory of Moral Sentiments*, Smith's first and only other book.

For much of the past two centuries, *The Theory of Moral Sentiments* has been overshadowed by his much better-known treatise on political economy. But things have changed recently. *The Theory of Moral Sentiments* has not only gained a wide academic following, but also attracted a striking amount of popular attention for a work of 18th-century ethics, as evident in its prominent recommendations by world leaders from British Prime Minister Gordon Brown to Chinese Premier Wen Jiabao.

What explains the attractions of *The Theory of Moral Sentiments* to these and others today? Among other things, the book describes a world in which exchanges of sympathy encourage individuals to cultivate the sense of propriety and the ethical virtues necessary to navigate life in a modern market society. It is a complex vision, one to which we cannot do full justice here. But we can note one of its most attractive features, namely its vision of human flourishing.

Smith presents this vision most clearly in the course of comparing justice and beneficence, in which he asks us to imagine two very different kinds of societies. In the first, he explains:

> All the members of human society stand in need of each others assistance, and are likewise exposed to mutual injuries. Where the necessary assistance is reciprocally afforded from love, from gratitude, from friendship, and esteem, the society flourishes and is happy. All the members of it are bound together by the agreeable bands of love and affection, and are, as it were, drawn to one common center of mutual good offices.[8]

He then compares this flourishing and happy society to a second type of society:

> But though the necessary assistance should not be afforded from such generous and disinterested motives, though among the different members of the society there should be no mutual love and affection, the society less happy and agreeable, will not necessarily be dissolved. Society may subsist among different men, as among different merchants, from a sense of its utility, without any mutual love or affection; and though no man in it should owe any obligation, or be bound in gratitude to any other, it may still be upheld by a mercenary exchange of good offices according to an agreed valuation.[9]

Smith's comparison of these two types of societies strikes to the very heart of his project—and indeed to the core concerns of political philosophy more generally.

Regarding Smith himself, these passages clearly reveal his view of what distinguishes the flourishing society: the society that "flourishes and is happy" is precisely that in which all are "bound together" into "one common center" by ties of "love and affection." It is fundamentally distinct from the society that in conspicuous contrast cannot be said to flourish, but rather merely "subsists"—that in which men, lacking mutual love and affection, maintain minimal ties based on a "mercenary exchange of good offices according to an agreed valuation."

What is Smith after in comparing these two societies in this way? Many have argued that his fundamental sympathies lie with the second type of society and not the first. And not without reason: in *The Wealth of Nations*, Smith praises the utility of exchange and criticizes benevolence in ways decidedly reminiscent of the second society described here.

Yet assuming that he somehow preferred the second society would do Smith an injustice. His description of it is of course painted in decidedly grim colors, clearly not meant to inspire enthusiasm. Indeed the cash nexus that allows this society to persist cannot seem anything but repellant when set next to—as Smith does—the warm bonds of love and friendship that define the best society.

This in turn brings us to the second reason why these passages are important—a reason that goes beyond their simple importance for Smith and speaks rather to the more general claims of political philosophy. At least since Aristotle, it has been customary for political philosophers to distinguish the best or ideal society from the best sort of society that can be realized in practice. Something like this distinction seems to be at work in Smith's comparison.

Smith was enough of a realist to know all too well the infinite difficulties inherent to any attempt to found the first and best sort of society here on earth; the ideal society of love asks more of us than what many of us are capable of. Our capacities and their limits compel us to live in societies of the second type rather than the first. At the same time, it would be fatal for us, amid our realism, to lose sight of the ideal that Smith aims to reawaken in us, even if that ideal cannot be fully realized in practice. Put in the terms of our main question, Smith's challenge to our world, a world built on the freedom to engage in "mercenary exchange," is to never forget that this alone cannot make us "happy."

Moral Flourishing

Our concerns to this point have largely focused on how Smith understood the flourishing society. Yet Smith, like Aristotle, was also concerned to describe the way in which an individual flourishes. To this end, he dedicated a large part of his book to the question of virtue—even going so far as to write, in the last year of his life, a completely new part of the book on the "character of virtue."

Smith's conception of virtue is itself of key significance for his project. It will also be of great interest to all concerned to define the virtues necessary for success in happiness in our own world—a world full of challenges and complications that render it quite different from the conditions of the ancient polis inhabited by Aristotle's gentleman. A full account of this theory, however, would again require much more space than is available here.[10] My hope instead is to end with a brief look at a third key passage in Smith on human flourishing—one particularly valuable for the way in which it connects the concepts of social flourishing to individual flourishing.

In this passage, Smith makes one of his boldest claims about human nature—a claim that itself subverts certain easy and common assumptions about his project. Smith's popular reputation as an ostensible champion of selfishness persists despite the repeated and conclusive debunking it has received from many scholars. Indeed, one need read only the first line of *The Theory of Moral Sentiments* to see how far he is from a defender of selfishness.

"How selfish soever man may be supposed," Smith begins, "there are evidently some principles in his nature, which interest him in the fortune of others, and render their happiness necessary to him, though he derives nothing from it except the pleasure of seeing it."[11] Smith's opening has deservedly received much scholarly attention, especially in recent years.

I want to focus on only one aspect of it here. At least one of Smith's aims, in starting his book this way, is to make clear from the outset that our happiness and the happiness of others around us are intimately bound up with each other. On some deep level, Smith in fact thinks that an individual can be happy and flourish only when others around him are happy and flourish.

This claim reappears several times in the book, perhaps nowhere more directly than in a second key passage on human flourishing. A few pages into the chapter that begins with the comparison, examined earlier, of the flourishing and merely subsisting societies, Smith again invokes the concept of human flourishing in a striking way:

> Man, it has been said, has a natural love for society, and desires that the union of mankind should be preserved for its own sake, and though he himself was to derive no benefit from it. The orderly and flourishing state of society is agreeable to him, and he takes delight in contemplating it. Its disorder and confusion on the contrary is the object of his aversion, and he is chagrined at whatever tends to produce it. He is sensible too that his own interest is connected with the prosperity of society, and that the happiness, perhaps the preservation of his existence, depends on its preservation.[12]

Smith makes a functionalist claim here: our existence depends on the existence of society. But another claim is also at work here, namely that our happiness depends on society's happiness. In this sense, he tells us, the "orderly and flourishing state of society" is something that we "delight in contemplating."

It is a striking claim and indeed one that suggests some sensitivity on Smith's part to the joys of contemplation and the claims of philosophy. But for now we need to limit ourselves to a single but important observation: namely that Smith thinks that we flourish when we see others around us flourish. Once again, Smith gives reasons for us to wonder whether our happiness can in fact be separated from the happiness of those around us.

Conclusion

Adam Smith, we can conclude, was not only a champion of economic freedom but also a champion of human flourishing. In his view, economic freedom was not a mere end in itself, but rather the indispensable means to a greater end, namely that of promoting human flourishing in its economic, political, and moral dimensions. In addition, Smith saw these three dimensions of human flourishing as all emanating from the same core principle: the superiority of a society joined together by the ties that bind to a society of disconnected and disaffected individuals.

But what implication does all of this have for us today? Much of course has happened in the quarter millennium since the publication of Smith's books. But in some sense Smith's concerns remain ours. In particular, much of what Smith most hoped for as a theorist of social order continues to be realized.

This is particularly evident in the remarkable progress that has been made in overcoming extreme global poverty. Recent predictions suggest that in the next 15 years we are likely to witness the virtual eradication of extreme global poverty, defined as living below $1.25 USD per day.[13] This accomplishment would constitute one of the most significant achievements of human civilization, one that reflects both the influence of Smith's ideas and the realization of one of his deepest hopes.

At the same time, this achievement is likely to bring in its wake a challenge of its own—a challenge that Smith's thoughts on human flourishing can help clarify. As we have seen, the core principle at the heart of Smith's various statements on the nature of human flourishing concerns the bonds that connect individuals to societies and different orders of society to each other when they flourish. One thus wonders: Is the society to come, the one in which extreme global poverty has been overcome, likely to be able to sustain these bonds?

The question may well come down to the degree to which our principal focus is soon likely to shift from concerns about poverty to concerns about inequality. Put bluntly, economic freedom, insofar as it has until now served to mitigate poverty, has promoted human flourishing. At the same time, economic freedom, were it to encourage inequality in the future, may diminish future human flourishing. If so, it may be that one of the most urgent tasks that liberals and conservatives each will soon have to face will be to explain whether and how an unequal society can hope to remain, in Smith's words, "bound together" around "one common center."

Notes

1. Excellent starting places for those who might wish to read further on Smith and his humane social vision include Nicholas Phillipson, *Adam Smith: An Enlightened Life* (New Haven, CT: Yale, 2010); Jerry Z. Muller, *Adam Smith in His Time and Ours* (Princeton: Princeton University Press, 1993); and Jerry Evensky, *Adam Smith's Moral Philosophy* (Cambridge: Cambridge University Press, 2005).

2. See, for example, Adam Smith, *An Inquiry into the Nature and Causes of the Wealth of Nations*, ed. R. H. Campbell and A. S. Skinner (Indianapolis: Liberty Fund, 1981), 1.11.m.8, 3.3.19–20, 4.7.b.30–31, and 5.8.58.

3. Smith, *The Wealth of Nations*, 1.8.36.

4. Ibid.

5. Adam Smith, *Lectures on Jurisprudence*, ed. R. L. Meek, D. D. Raphael, and P. G. Stein (Indianapolis: Liberty Fund, 1982), A, iv.33.

6. Smith, *Wealth of Nations*, 1.1.10.

7. Craig Smith, "Adam Smith: Left or Right?" *Political Studies* 61 (2013): 784–98. This debate is furthered in two recent essays: Samuel Fleischacker, "Adam Smith and the Left" in *Adam Smith: His Life, Thought, and Legacy*,

ed. Ryan Patrick Hanley (Princeton: Princeton University Press, 2016); and James Otteson, "Adam Smith and the Right" in *Adam Smith: His Life, Thought, and Legacy*, ed. Ryan Patrick Hanley (Princeton, NJ: Princeton University Press, 2016).

8. Adam Smith, *The Theory of Moral Sentiments*, ed. D. D. Raphael and A. L. Macfie (Indianapolis: Liberty Fund, 1982), 2.2.3.1.

9. Ibid., 2.2.3.2.

10. For a more detailed overviews of Smith's theory of virtue, see Hanley, "Smith and Virtue," in *The Oxford Handbook of Adam Smith*, ed. Christopher Berry, Craig Smith, and Maria Pia Paganelli (Oxford: Oxford University Press, 2013); and Hanley, *Adam Smith and the Character of Virtue* (Cambridge: Cambridge University Press, 2009).

11. Smith, *Theory of Moral Sentiments*, 1.1.1.1.

12. Ibid., 2.2.3.6.

13. For an overview, see US Agency for International Development, *Getting to Zero: A Discussion Paper on Ending Extreme Poverty*, November 21, 2013, http://www.usaid.gov/sites/default/files/documents/1870/USAID-Extreme-Poverty-Discussion-Paper.pdf.

Economic Liberty and Human Flourishing: Kant on Society, Citizenship, and Redistributive Justice

SUSAN MELD SHELL
Boston College

The topic of Immanuel Kant on economic liberty and human flourishing might seem a short one indeed: justice, as Kant famously put it, has nothing do with the end of achieving happiness. [8: 289–90][1] And it is our failure to understand the distinction that opens the floodgates to paternalism and tyranny.

This said, if one understands "flourishing" to include more than material well-being, Kant does have something enlightening to say, perhaps uniquely. That subject is best approached, given limited time, by a consideration of two related topics that he does discuss in some detail: the justice of redistribution on the one hand and the nature of republican citizenship on the other.

Scholars have long been divided on the redistributive implications of Kant's theory of justice. On the one hand, there is a prominent "libertarian" reading (including that of von Humbolt, Hayek, and Nozick, among others), according to which the function of the state is mainly to defend and maintain private market outcomes. On the other hand, Kant's work has also inspired, almost from its inception, a more "social democratic" reading (such as that of Fichte and Hermann Cohen). I will argue that both readings ignore Kant's actual justification of the state's duty to tax the wealthy to relieve the poor: namely, the "end," on the part of the "general will of the people," to "unite into a society that is to maintain itself perpetually." [6: 326] In what follows I will attempt to spell out the meaning of this phrase, with a view to providing an alternative (limited) defense of contemporary liberal democratic welfare policies. I will also consider the larger question of what, according to Kant, it means to be a full-fledged member of the political community: i.e., an "active citizen" as distinguished from a mere, if still vitally necessary, "participant," and what, if anything, governments should do to facilitate such membership.

Kant on Redistributive Justice: Current Approaches

Current approaches to Kant on distributive justice roughly divide between libertarian "minimalism" (with or without insistence on a safety net) and some version of state welfarism. Although the former was until recently the dominant view (at least going by the not-too-distant past),[2] state-welfarist approaches have recently become increasingly popular. These approaches divide, roughly, between those that derive a right or duty on the part of the state to make provision for the poor from some version of the duty of beneficence,[3] and those, increasingly influential, that derive that right or duty from a citizen's innate right to external freedom understood as independence from the arbitrary will [*Willkür*] of others.[4]

Additionally, scholars from both minimalist and welfarist camps have found reasons to contest a distinction on Kant's part, with potential distributive implications, between active and passive citizenship: the former group, because that distinction seems inconsistent with the formalistic account of equal liberty they favor, the latter because allowance for the category of passive citizenship seems inconsistent with the independence to which citizens are innately entitled.[5] As I will argue below, both interpretations miss something essential in Kant's own treatment of the twin issues of redistribution and citizenship. That conclusion is supported both by a careful reading of the few passages in which Kant discusses these themes directly, and consideration of the broader implications of his understanding of public right both in the ideal case and with a view to its empirical actualization.

Relevant Kantian Texts

Supporters of the minimalist view can find apparent corroboration for their reading in a number of texts, including a series of passages from the essay *Theory and Practice* (1793), which stress the juridical irrelevance of material inequality as such, along with all other considerations pertaining to the actual happiness of citizens.

> The whole concept of an external right [*Rechts*] is derived entirely from the concept of *freedom* in the mutual external relationships of human beings, and has nothing to do with the end which all men have by nature (i.e., the aim of achieving happiness) or with the recognised means of attaining this end. And thus the latter end must on no account interfere as a determinant with the laws governing external right. *Right* is the restriction of each individual's freedom so that it harmonizes with the freedom of everyone else (in so far as this is possible within the terms of a general law). And *public right* is the distinctive quality of the *external laws* which make this constant harmony possible. Since every restriction of freedom through the arbitrary will of another party is termed *coercion,* it follows that a civil constitution is a relationship among free men who are subject to coercive laws, while they retain their freedom within the general union with their fellows. Such is the requirement of pure reason, which legislates *a priori,* regardless of all empirical ends (which can all be summed up under the general heading of happiness). Men have different views on the empirical end of happiness and what it consists of, so that as far as happiness is concerned, their will cannot be brought under any common principle nor thus under any external law harmonising with the freedom of everyone. [8: 289–90]

It would seem to follow that the "freedom," "equality," and "independence" that are constitutive of the concept of citizenship have no necessary relation to distributive issues as such. Juridical equality, as Kant here insists, is quite consistent with the greatest degree and kind of material inequality, be it physical or mental:

This uniform equality of human beings as subjects of a state is . . . perfectly consistent with the utmost inequality of the mass in the degree of its possessions, whether these take the form of physical or mental superiority over others, or of fortuitous external property and of particular rights (of which there may be many) with respect to others. Thus the welfare of the one depends very much on the will of the other (the poor depending on the rich), the one must obey the other (as the child its parents or the wife her husband), the one serves (the laborer) while the other pays, etc. Nevertheless, they are all equal as subjects *before the law,* which, as the pronouncement of the general will, can only be single in form, and which concerns the form of right and not the material or object in relation to which I possess rights. [8: 291–92]

The anti-redistributivist tenor of these remarks is echoed in the introduction to Kant's later, and arguably more definitive, *Doctrine of Right* (1797), which defines right as an "external" relation among wills [*Willküren*], a relation that not only entirely abstracts from the matter of the will (or the end each has in view) but also ignores mere "needs" or "wishes" (i.e., desires not accompanied by consciousness of the means [*Vermögen*] to bring about their object). [6: 230, 213] The minimalist reading finds further apparent support in the richly elaborated section on "private right." According to that account, external property, whether acquired originally (i.e., where there is no previous owner) or through voluntary exchange, cannot be rightfully taken away or otherwise made use of without the owner's consent, however great the need of others.[6] Kant's accompanying systematic treatment of private right in all its possible conceptual permutations gives added weight to the presumption that market outcomes are intrinsically legitimate, and that any argument for redistributive adjustment would bear a very heavy justificatory burden. That impression is seemingly confirmed by Kant's later claim, in introducing the notion of "public right," that the laws regarding "mine and thine" are "formally the same," whether one is speaking of civil society or of the state of nature:

If one would not want [wollte] to recognize any acquisition as rightful [rechtlich] even provisionally prior to entering into the civil condition, the civil condition itself would be impossible. For according to their form, the laws regarding mine and thine in the state of nature contain the very same thing they prescribe in the civil condition insofar as these are thought according to pure concepts of reason: only that in the latter case the conditions are stated under which these can arrive at execution [Ausübung] (in conformity with distributive justice).— Thus if external mine and thine were not given even *provisionally* the state of nature, there would also be given no duty of right concerning it, and hence no command to exit from it. [6: 312–13]

At the same time, Kant himself is quite specific about the positive authorization of the state to tax the rich for the relief of the impoverished, suggesting that a minimalist reading that wishes to remain true to Kant's text must, at least, allow for the provision of a "safety net" for those unable to provide for their most immediate needs:

To the supreme commander there belongs *indirectly*, i.e., as taking over the duty of the people, the right to impose taxes on the people for its (the people's) own preservation, to wit: *institutions for the poor, foundling homes* and *church organizations* usually called charitable or pious institutions. [6: 325–26]

As Kant proceeds to explain:

The general will of the people [allgemeine Volkswille] has united itself . . . into a society [Gesellschaft] which should maintain itself perpetually, and has to that end subjected itself to inner state authority in order to maintain those members of this society who are not able to maintain themselves [die es selbst nicht vermögen]. On a state level [Von Staatswegen], therefore, government is justified in necessitating those with means [die Vermögenden] to provide the means [Mittel] of sustenance to those who are unable to provide for their most necessary natural needs: because the existence [Existenz] of those with means is at the same time, as an act of submission, under the protection and

provision of the commonwealth that is necessary to their [own] existence [*Dasein*], through which they have made themselves obliged
to contribute what is theirs to maintaining their fellow citizens, on
which obligation the state now grounds its right. [6: 326]

This terse and syntactically complex passage has lent itself to a
variety of interpretations. Some read what Kant here calls the "duty
of the people" as one of benevolence, which the state subsequently
adopts.[7] Others extract from it an unenforceable right to sustenance grounded in the general will by which the state is originally
constituted, and in which individuals renounce their right to make
use ad libitum of objects external to their own bodies in exchange
for state provision for their bare existence.[8] Still others take it as an
argument for a safety net based on the state's requirements for its
own survival.[9]

Taken literally, however—or so I will argue—the passage yields a
series of claims that do not strictly conform to any of the now standard interpretations.

1. The "duty of the people" here at issue is not a duty of benevolence but, as Kant immediately goes on to explain, one arising
   from the juridically constitutive act itself, and hence a duty of
   right rather than (mere) ethics.

2. This duty does not derive from the supposed right of those
   in need to state support (as is sometimes urged), but on the
   collective "end" intended by the people's general will in sub-
   mitting itself to state authority.

The end here at issue is not the ongoing existence of the *state*
(which was the subject of the preceding section of Kant's text
[6: 323–25]), but that of an "ever-enduring" *society*, which differs
from the state, as Kant earlier makes clear when he takes issue with
Achenwall on just this point [6: 242, 306].

As to the precise difference between the civil and the social union
(or, alternatively expressed, the merely *social* dimension of that civil
union), Kant offers the following clarifying remarks: a social state,

which can also be called "artificial," remains "a state of nature" so long as law generally, and distributive justice in particular, are lacking.[10] The relevant contrast is thus not between the state of nature and that of society (however artificial) but between the state of nature and the civil union or juridical condition. Social unions can be compatible with rights [gesetzmässig] even in a state of nature (as is the case with spousal, parental, and domestic societies in general). [6: 306] Such rights-compatible societies are, however, specifically distinguished from civil unions in at least the following two ways: (1) unlike the civil union, there is no duty to enter a (private) society (like the family) [6: 306] and (2) unlike the civil union, which involves relations of subordination between superior and inferior, society is a partnership involving relations of coordination among equals. Thus:

> The civil union (unio civilis) cannot well be called a society [Gesellschaft]; because between the commander (imperans) and the subject (subditus) there is no partnership (Mitgenossenschaft). They are not social fellows [Gesellen];[11] rather, one is subordinated to, not coordinated with, the other. And those who are coordinated with one another must regard themselves as equals, as they stand under the same common laws. It is thus less the case that this union [Verein] is a society than that it makes one. [6: 306–7]

It seems reasonable to conclude that unlike private societies (such as the family), the public society here at issue is a creature of the state, not merely in the sense of depending upon the state for its maintenance and defense, but also in owing its existence to the self-constitutive juridical act by which the state itself is formed. [6: 314; 315–6; cf, 320n]

Political society in the sense at issue in Section C (on the "police power") is, then, that dimension of the civil union whose constituents participate not as co-legislative citizens or "members" [Glied] of the "commonwealth" [gemeinen Wesen] but as "subjects" who are equal to one another in their common submission to civic law (or to the head of state as their "commander") [6: 314]. It is on this plane that those citizens he earlier described as "passive" (a topic which will be taken up again below) participate as equal "members" of "society"—the natural or quasi-natural matrix, one might say, absent which the state as form would lack the matter necessary to its own ongoing this-worldly existence. Such a society, as one might surmise, is a necessary concession to our status as embodied rational beings who must both produce and reproduce the natural conditions of their own ongoing existence, both individual and collective, if they are to carry out the end intended by the people's general will: namely, the people's own existence as an ever-enduring society.

Read in this light, the duty of the people is twofold: at once individual and collective, arising from a shared "intention" to form a society, along with the accompanying *Akt* by which each is reborn, so to speak, as a citizen [6: 343], owing his/her existence to the protection and provision of the commonwealth. As member of the general will, in other words, each wills his *own* existence as citizen only insofar as he also, and equally, wills the civic existence of every other member of the people.[12]

In sum, the duty of the people that is taken over by the state and that authorizes the state to impose coercive taxes on those with means is *not* a duty of beneficence (an *ethical* duty that is, as such, unenforceable) but one of right. And the immediate *end* of the state action thus authorized is neither the welfare of the people (which would be paternalism) nor the state's *own* preservation (as in Kant's earlier discussion of the state in its capacity as "supreme proprietor" [6: 323–25]), but the preservation of "society." Society, in this sense, is both a creature of the state (unlike wholly private societies such as families) and its necessary complement, for reasons that will be further explored below.

That the state's authorization to tax the wealthy to provide for the needy is explicitly associated—in the only passage that directly addresses the issue of redistribution—with the ongoing preservation of society as such calls into question some recent efforts to ground Kant's justification for such policies in the individual's innate right to independence from the individual wills of others, an independence essentially threatened, according to proponents of that argument, by a state of material want.[13] Their argument is rendered still more doubtful by Kant's urging, in the passage that immediately follows, that redistributive policies be framed so as to discourage those relieved from becoming "lazy" or otherwise unjustly imposing on the people generally:

> It may be asked whether provision for the poor ought to be administered out of *current contributions*—and this by direct assessment rather than by begging, which is closely akin to robbery—so that every age should maintain its own, or whether this were better done gradually by means of *permanent funds* and charitable institutions, such as widows' homes, hospitals, etc. The former arrangement must be held as the only one that is conformable to the right of the state, from which no one who has to live can withdraw: for (unlike pious institutions) it does not, even if the number of the poor grows, become a means of acquisition [*Erwerbmittel*] for lazy human beings, and thus become through the government an unjust burden on the people. [6: 326]

Kant's stated concern in the above passage is not with assuring the independence of the poor (as might be anticipated on the basis of the Weinrib/Ripstein reading) but in preventing lazy individuals from taking unjust advantage of the people as a whole.[14]

Still, if neither the argument from the duty of beneficence, nor the argument from the innate right to independence, seems to do full justice to Kant's actual claims, Kant's own argument is not stated with all the clarity that one might wish: the precise relation between the specified end, namely an ever-enduring society (or, alternatively, people), and the means, namely provision through taxation of the wealthy for support of those unable to satisfy their most basic natural needs, remains obscure. If the end is merely the preservation of society in general, does the duty of the people apply to *each* and *every* needy person, are merely enough to ensure the perpetuation of society?[15] And how is this end to be weighted against other juridical goals, such as maintaining the state?

At one level, what Kant means by the "preservation of the people" [6: 325–26] might seem obvious enough: without a strong and healthy population, the state cannot perform its essential functions of assuring to each what is his/hers.[16] The state's legitimate interest in a maintaining a large and healthy population is, indeed, mentioned elsewhere in the *Rechtslehre*, for example in Kant's treatment of punishment and clemency, where the need to preserve the population [*Volksmenge*] is enough to modify a demand for capital punishment that would otherwise be categorical. [6: 334]

Still, that more is intended by the term "society" than the population in a merely natural sense is suggested even there: Kant's stated concern is less with the depletion of able bodies than with the morally dulling effect that would be produced by the spectacle of massive slaughter, however fitting from a strictly punitive perspective.[17] And the example is itself presented as one of those rare "cases of necessity" [6: 334] in which immediate, seemingly empirical requirements momentarily override the strict demands of justice.

To better appreciate what Kant means by the preservation of society in the sense that is here juridically most pertinent—the sort of society, in other words, that derives, directly and necessarily, from the people's general will, and gives rise, in turn, to their duty to preserve the needy [6: 326]—it proves helpful to examine his discussion of citizenship. For, as I will argue, it is in Kant's treatment of the contrast between civil persons in their capacity as co-legislative citizens and [civil] persons in their capacity as subjects that the contours of society, and with it, the function and limits of economic redistribution, emerge most clearly.

Kant's Dual Account of Citizenship

One of Kant's most disturbing juridical claims, for modern readers, lies in his distinction between active and passive citizens, only the former of whom may vote or otherwise actively participate in the management of state affairs.[18] Kant's derivation of the state's lawgiving authority [*Gewalt*] from the united will of all the people [6: 313], and related identification of the "essence" of citizenship with lawgiving [6: 314], makes that distinction all the more puzzling.

That puzzlement is partly allayed by taking into account the political/historical context, and—in particular—the fact that Kant's categories of "active" and "passive" citizen are lifted almost verbatim from the French Constitution of 1791, following the recommendations of Abbe Siéyès. In adopting these categories—as Kant's contemporary audience would surely have recognized—Kant was also laying down a political marker in favor of the French constitutional moderates and against radicals like Robespierre, who was closely identified with the cause of universal suffrage.[19] To call for universal suffrage, in such a context, would be close to endorsement of the Terror that had quickly followed Robespierre's rise.

Siéyès' recommendations, originally penned in 1789, and subsequently adopted by the National Assembly, had called for a graduated civic status, ascending from that of "passive" citizens, who were to enjoy protection of life, liberty, and property, to that of "active" citizens, who were also to be granted increasing "political rights" corresponding to their wealth and other productive contributions to "society."[20] The effectual threshold of active citizenship adopted by the National Assembly was payment of a tax equivalent to three days' labor.

To be sure, Kant's own treatment of active and passive citizenship diverges from French practice and/or the recommendations of Siéyès, in a number of important ways. First, whereas the National Assembly, following Siéyès, had made the right to vote conditional upon possession of a degree of taxable (productively derived) wealth, Kant rests that right, more formally and abstractly, on what he calls "self-subsistence" [Selbstständigkeit].[21] Second, whereas Siéyès had defined the "nation" as a "society" or "body of associates living under common laws and represented by the same legislative assembly," Kant, as we earlier saw, specifically distinguishes the people qua "society" from the commonwealth [gemeinen Wesen], or state, by which that society is, as Kant puts it, "made." [6: 306–7] Finally, whereas Siéyès includes within the "nation" only members of the productive class, or "third estate" (as distinguished from the non-productive first and second estates—i.e., the clergy and nobility—or anyone laying claim to exceptional political privilege), Kant includes all willing to join in constituting a people.

The essential attributes of a citizen, according to Kant, are (1) "freedom" in the sense of obeying no law other than one to which one has consented, (2) 'equality" in the sense of regarding no one among the people as superior to oneself in moral capacity to bind others, and (3) "self-reliance" or "self-subsistence" in the sense of owing one's preservation to one's own "rights" and "forces" as member of the commonwealth:[22]

> The members of such a society (*societas civilis*), i.e., a state, united for giving law, are called *citizens* (*cives*), and the rightful attributes of a citizen, inseparable from his essence [*Wesen*] (as such) are lawful *freedom*, obeying no other law than one to which he has given his consent [*Beistimmung*]; civil *equality*, recognizing no one superior among the *people* as having the moral power [*Vermögen*] to juridically bind him in a way that he could not in turn bind the other; and third, the attribute of civil *self-subsistence* [*Selbständigkeit*], of being able to thank for his existence and maintenance not the Willkür of another among the people, but his own rights and forces as member of the commonwealth [*gemeinen Wesen*], it following from this his civil personality, not needing to be represented by another in matters concerning rights. [6: 314]

Kant's verbal linkage between the "essence" [*Wesen*] of the citizen and the commonwealth as, literally, the "common essence" [*gemeinen Wesen*] drives home the integrative character of civic *Selbständigkeit*. The citizen is self-subsistent not in an autarkical sense but only in relation to and as integral member of the whole.[23]

That all members of the people are not "self-subsistent" in this sense "makes necessary" a distinction, however, between active and passive citizens, only the former of whom may vote or otherwise actively participate in managing affairs of state.

> The qualification to be a citizen is constituted only by the capacity [*Fähigkeit*] for voting [*Stimmgebung*]; this, however, presupposes the self-sufficiency of one among the people who would be not only a part [*Theil*] of the commonwealth but also a member [*Glied*] of it, that is to say, an acting [*handelnder*] part in community with others from his own Willkür. The latter quality, however, makes necessary

the distinction of *active* [*activen*] from *passive* citizens, even though the concept of the latter seems to stand in contradiction with that of a citizen in general. [6: 314][24]

Kant is sensitive to the difficulty, bordering on contradiction, that this "necessity" poses, given his essential definition of a citizen as a "law-giving" member of the "state" understood as a *societas civilis*. [6: 313–14] Kant responds with a series of clarifying examples of those who are only fit to be passive citizens:

The journeyman [*Geselle*] of a merchant or a craftsman; the domestic servant [*Dienstbote*] (not one who stands in service [*Dienste*] to the state); the minor (natural or civil); all women, and generally anyone who is compelled [*genoetigigt*] to maintain his existence (nurture and protection) not through his own operation [*Betrieb*] but according to the arrangements [*Befuegung*] of another (other than the state) lacks civil personality, and his existence is so to speak only inherence.— The woodcutter whom I employ in my yard, the blacksmith in India who goes house to house with iron with his hammer, anvil and bellows to work with iron, in comparison with the European carpenter or blacksmith who can place the products of his labor publicly up for sale as wares; the house tutor in comparison with the schoolteacher; the tenant farmer in comparison with the lease-hold farmer, and so forth, are mere handy-men [*Handlanger*] of the commonwealth, because they must be under the direction or protection of other individuals and thus possess no civil self-subsistence. [6: 314]

What each of these figures has in common is a shared need to be "under the direction or protection" of another. Whereas Siéyès had considered such a condition akin to slavery,[25] Kant himself *distinguishes* slavery, which is a fundamental violation of the innate right of each to be his own master (*sui iuris*) [6: 237–38], from dependence in the sense here intended, a dependence entirely consistent with that innate right, according to Kant, so long as it is based either on one's natural status as a minor (as with children), or arrangements arising from one's own choice, and limited by the rights of humanity

in one's own person. [6: 276–284, 285].[26] (An additional, final pro-
viso, namely that nothing stand in the way of passive citizens "working their way up" to active status, will be taken up below [6: 315]).
Indeed, it is only through due recognition of this innate right to freedom and equality—a right that those who enter into such relations
of dependence are incapable of forfeiting—that the state is possible
at all. Thus:

> This dependence on the will of another and inequality [implicit in
> passive citizenship] is . . . in no way opposed to the freedom and
> equality [of such citizens] as human beings who together constitute a
> people; on the contrary, it is only on conformity to the conditions of
> [this freedom and equality] that this people can constitute a state and
> enter into a civil constitution. In this constitution, however, to have
> the right to vote [Stimmgebung], i.e., to be a citizen of the state and
> not merely an associate [Staatsgenosse], for this all do not qualify with
> equal right. For from their right to demand of all others that they be
> treated/handled [behandelt] according to natural laws of freedom and
> equality as passive parts [Theil] of the state there does not follow the
> right to handle themselves [behandeln] as active members [Glieder] of
> the state itself, to organize [organisiren] or cooperate [mitzuwirken] in
> the introduction of specific laws; it only follows that whatever posi-
> tive laws the state citizens might vote for not be opposed to [zuwider
> sein] the natural laws of freedom and the corresponding equality of
> all among the people: namely, being able to work one's way up [empor
> arbeiten] from this passive condition to the active one. [6: 315]

Kant's own distinction between active and passive citizenship
might thus be put as follows: On the one hand, the passive citizen, like all citizens, participates in that general will by which all are
united to give a law in which "each wills for all and all for each," a
law that is necessarily just in accordance with the principle that "no
one can do himself an injustice." On the other hand, the "organized"
power [Gewalt] thereby authorized, through which subsequent positive laws are to be introduced, is to be conceived, on Kant's view,
as a separate community in its own right.[27] The members of that

community, unlike the general members of society at large, have what he here calls "civil personality" [*bürgerliche Personalität*] [6: 314], as distinguished from the "moral personality," both internal and external, that no human being is capable of giving up. [6: 223][28]

In sum, qua *citizen*, the passive citizen is a full-fledged member of the people and with it the general will by which the people both constitute the state and subject themselves to the latter's threefold authority [*Gewalt*]: legislative, executive, and judicial. [6: 315–16] Qua *passive* citizen, however, he is subject to the legislative authority to which he has ideally given his consent as member of the general will, without, unlike the active citizen, playing an ongoing role in organizing or otherwise "cooperating" in "the introduction of specific laws." [6: 314–15]

Citizenship and Redistributive Justice

If this is indeed the right way to understand Kant's distinction between active and passive citizenship, how might it bear on issues of redistributive justice and, in particular, the duty/authorization to compel those with means to provide for those in need? And in what way, if at all, might the requirement that passive citizens "be able to work their way up" to active citizenship (if the category of passive citizenship is to remain consistent with a citizen's innate right to freedom and equality) translate into the duty or authorization of the state to actively enable those in a position of dependence to thus work their way up?

One answer that does not seem satisfactory, at least if one wishes to remain true to Kant's own words, is the recent and increasingly influential view that dependence *as such* represents a violation of the innate right to independence from the will of others, a violation that the state is accordingly obliged to set right by vigorous redistributive intervention. For, as we have seen, by Kant's own lights there is nothing intrinsically wrong (contrary to right) with a condition of economic or personal dependence, so long as it arises from one's own choice and/or (temporary) natural incapacity, such as youth or imbecility.[29]

I would suggest, instead, the following two-tiered approach. The **first** stems from the duty of the people to provide for the most basic natural needs of those who, through no fault of their own,[30] cannot provide for themselves, either "self-sufficiently" (in the manner of active citizens) or through other voluntary arrangements (e.g., by temporarily "hiring out" to another the "use of [their own] forces" [6: 285, 330]). Such provision might be likened to other policies with redistributive implications, policies that Kant might endorse on similar grounds. Given flexible and rising standards of what it means to have one's basic natural needs unmet (e.g., lack of access to inoculation against common infectious diseases), such provision might, indeed, prove quite expansive, including access to adequate health care services, decent housing, nutritional support, and so on, so long as care was taken that such provision not become a "means of acquisition" for the lazy and thereby unjustly burden the people as a whole.

The **second** basis for redistributive policies stems from the requirement that nothing prevent passive citizens from "working their way up" to active status. On a "minimalist" reading, to be sure, this would demand no more than that there be no legal bars to such advancement (of a sort that still existed in contemporary Prussia, where serfdom had not yet been completely abolished, and noble status remained necessary for placement in the upper military ranks, as would remain the case until the end of World War I.) But that Kant himself had more in mind is suggested by his frequent flirtations with the idea of universal state-supported education—a policy that had, in principle if not in practice, been in place in Prussia since the early 18th century. His objection to state, as opposed to privately supported, education was based not on the worry that it might unjustly burden taxpayers, but on the likelihood of it resulting, under current political conditions, in popular moral and religious indoctrination inimical to the cause of freedom. That children had a *right* to education—a right directed, in the first instance, against their parents—Kant had no doubt, and it seems reasonable to assume that he would have urged, in cases in which parents could not fulfill this obligation, that the state make it available, either indirectly or directly.

At the same time, the *content* of the education that Kant favored (as described in his Lectures on Pedagogy) suggests the limits he would probably have placed on positive state efforts to help citizens advance from passive to active status: namely, that such policies not unwittingly subvert a citizen's *own* efforts to become able to maintain himself through his own forces. It here becomes especially important to distinguish *Selbständigkeit* in the sense of being self-supporting from "independence" as understood by contemporary scholars (following the work of Phillip Pettit, Quentin Skinner, and others).[31] Whereas "independence" (the term commonly used to translate *Selbständigkeit*) places the emphasis, especially if understood in Pettit's sense, on freedom *from* domination by another's will, Kant himself places the emphasis on the positive ability to be "self-supporting" [9: 486, 491–92], i.e., to rationally manage one's own affairs on the basis of one's own resources [*Vermögen*], whether material or mental, as a member of the commonwealth.

But "to be one's own master" in a juridical sense is *not* the same, in Kant's understanding, as self-subsistence. Savages, for example, may enjoy independence in the sense of freedom from domination by another will (and are properly *sui iuis*) and yet manifestly lack the qualities necessary for *Selbständigkeit* as Kant himself defines it. To be self-subsistent in this sense is, in Kant's own words, to be "an acting [*handelnder*] part in community with others from [one's] own Willkür." One who is thus qualified "can thank for his existence and maintenance" his "own rights and forces as member of the commonwealth," rather than depending another *Willkür*, or capacity for choice, in the acquisition and deployment of the means needed for his own support. [6: 314; cf. 213]

Such qualities include not only skills and discipline for which culture and civilization are necessary, but also a certain strength of character that can only be acquired through personal effort, be it (to cite the ideal case) during a properly guided childhood and youth, in the manner sketched in Kant's own *Lectures on Pedagogy*, or otherwise.[32]

Understood in this light, Kant's distinction between active and passive citizenship not only suggests certain necessary limits of any positive policies in support of citizens' ascent from passive to active status; it also sheds light on Kant's argument for the duty of the people, and related authorization of the state, to compel the wealthy to provide for those who are truly needy (i.e., who, through no fault of their own, cannot meet their most basic natural needs). What is juridically pertinent about such a condition, on the reading I am urging, is not the immediate threat to life as such, the right to which, as some have claimed, cannot be given up on entering civil society; nor is it the inaccessibility of external means that would have been available in a state of nature in which all acquired property is merely provisional. As Lebar has noted, the means available to individuals for their individual existence and maintenance are likely far greater in a juridical condition than in a state of nature. Nor is it dependence on the *Willkür* of others (e.g., to offer one employment), once all the accessible land is taken, contrary to innate right as such; for dependence in this sense is the fate of *any* member of society who does not elect to be a hermit. (The head of General Motors is dependent on the *Willkür* of his customers, etc.)[33] If the (alleged) threat to individual independence was indeed the ground of the people's duty to support the needy, one might expect Kant to mention it here, but no such argument appears either here or elsewhere in the text.

The pertinence of that condition of need lies, rather, in its relation to the end and act of the juridically constitutive general will, which unanimously intended the ongoing existence of the people. It is not his own individual existence that each member of the general will must be presumed to have had in view, but his own existence only insofar as it counted neither more nor less than that of others. The duty of the wealthy to those in need is thus one of reciprocity: the wealthy have already enjoyed no less benefit from the protection of the commonwealth than they are now obliged to give. This reciprocal dependence is precisely in keeping with the equality of rich and poor as subject members of "society" in general, as distinguished from "civil society" or the "commonwealth," in whose necessitating authority only those capable of rationally managing their own affairs are fit to actively participate.[34]

A final suggestion: Kant may well have conceived of passive citizenship as a useful form of civil and moral education, at least potentially, particularly for those without access to the sort of ideal youthful education that he favored. This may, indeed, have been true for Kant himself, who served as a house tutor until the age of 31, remaining on excellent terms with one of families for the rest of his life. It is arguably by serving in such posts that Kant, himself from a modest artisanal background, acquired the urbanity and other social skills that won him the title "elegant master" when he last began to lecture at the university in 1755. (He would not assume a regular university post for another 15 years.)

Indeed, if, as Kant elsewhere insists, true maturity, both civil and moral, rarely occurs before age 40, then a prolonged state of civil "journeymanship"[35] may be unavoidable, whatever one's actual material means.

If this suggestion has merit, passive citizenship (in an extended sense) might have its own necessary uses, especially given the imperfect state of education.[36] Abraham Lincoln may have had something similar in mind when he hoped that employees who made up the ranks of what was then called "free labor" might at some point in their lives have the opportunity to work for themselves—at some point, but not immediately.[37] And that aspiration lives on in the dream, not only American, of "being one's own boss," a status not generally thought inconsistent with starting out as an employee under the direction and management of others. I am far from urging that we revert to the sort of limited suffrage embraced by Kant, French moderates like Siéyès, and the framers of the US Constitution. Still, the remarkably low voting rate among those who lack self-subsistence in a roughly Kantian sense might give one pause. Perhaps this is less deplorable, from a civil and moral point of view, than most liberal democrats today are wont to think. What is crucial, from a Kantian point of view (suitably updated), is that any such state of apprenticeship be genuinely conducive to the acquisition of *Selbständigkeit*, or what might be called civic character, within the limits of the human condition—a condition that necessarily includes relations of dependency (on the part of the young, the very old, and those who, for whatever reason, do not will or want to be an active member of the commonwealth).

Notes

1. Immanuel Kant, *Gesammelte Schriften*, ed. Preussischen Akademie der Wissenschaften (Berlin-Brandenburg Akademie der Wissenschaften) (Berlin: Georg Reimer; Berlin: Walter de Gruyter, 1900–), 8: 289–90. Bracketed references cite this edition of Kant's works; translations are by the author.

2. See, for example, Robert Nozick, *Anarchy, State and Utopia* (New York: Basic Books, 1974); Jeffrie J. Murphy, *Kant: The Philosophy of Right* (Macon, GA: Mercer University Press, 1994); Friedrich A. Hayek, *Law, Legislation and Liberty*, vol. 2, *The Mirage of Social Justice* (Chicago: University of Chicago Press, 1969); with some qualification, Mark LeBar, "Kant on Welfare," *Canadian Journal of Philosophy* 29, no. 2 (1999): 225–50; Wolfgang Kersting, "Kant's Concept of the State," in *Essays on Kant's Political Philosophy*, ed. Howard Lloyd Williams (Cardiff, UK: University of Wales Press, 1992); and B. Sharon Byrd and Joachim Hruschka, *Kant's Doctrine of Right: A Commentary* (Cambridge, UK: Cambridge University Press, 2012).

3. See, for example, Onora O'Neill, "Rights, Obligations and World Hunger," in *Global Ethics: Seminal Essays*, ed. Thomas W. Pogge (Oxford, UK: Blackwell, 2008), 139–54.

4. See, for example, Ernest J. Weinrib, "Poverty and Property in Kant's System of Rights," *Notre Dame Law Review* 78, no. 3 (2003): 795–828; and Arthur Ripstein, *Force and Freedom* (Cambridge, MA: Harvard University Press, 2009); cf. Sarah Holtman, "Kantian Justice and Poverty Relief," *Kant-Studien* 95, no. 1 (March 2004): 86–106. For a thorough and insightful discussion of the recent literature on issues of redistribution in Kant, see Sorin Baiasu, "Kant's Justification of Welfare," *Diametros* 39 (March 2014): 1–28.

5. See, for example, Helen Varden, "Kant and Dependency Relations: Kant on the State's Right to Redistribute Resources to Protect the Rights of Dependents," *Dialogue* 45, no. 2 (2006): 257–84; and Alice Pinheiro Walla, "Human Nature and the Right to Coerce in Kant's *Doctrine of Right*," *Archiv für Geschichte der Philosophie* 96, no. 1 (2014): 126–39.

6. This is not to say that someone who uses them in the state of nature, in which all acquired property is merely "provisional," necessarily does their owner a "wrong." The contentious question of how to understand the force and limits of "provisional" ownership cannot detain us here.

7. See, for example, O'Neill, "Rights, Obligations and World Hunger"; and Allen D. Rosen, *Kant's Theory of Justice* (Ithaca, NY: Cornell University Press, 1993).

8. See, for example, Weinrib, "Poverty and Property in Kant's System of Rights"; and Ripstein, *Force and Freedom.*

9. See Lebar, "Kant on Welfare."

10. In distinguishing between the civil and the social in this way, Kant *may* have had in mind a similar distinction drawn by Abbe Siéyès, with whose work Kant seems to have been generally familiar. On the relation between Kant and Siéyès, see below.

11. *Geselle* generally means "companion" or "comrade." *Handwerkgeselle* is a technical term for "journeyman." Kant himself uses *Geselle* to mean "journeyman." [6: 314]

12. On this point, see also Howard Williams, "Kant and Libertarianism," in *Kant on Practical Justification*, ed. Mark Timmons and Sorin Baiasu (Oxford, UK: Oxford University Press, 2013).

13. A good deal more would have to be said to meet the Weinrib/Ripstein argument, which has many powerful features. On the face of things, however, their approach comes perilously close to the argument Kant explicitly rejects with respect to capital punishment: namely that individuals could not rationally consent to join a juridical community if it meant consenting to the loss of one's own life. [6: 335] Kant does speak elsewhere of the claim of the desperately needy arising from their status as human beings or, alternatively, as "citizens of the world," i.e., shipwreck survivors or others who unwillingly arrive on foreign shores. That the rights of such survivors include only temporary food and shelter, rather than a right to settle, further suggests that the duty to relieve that is at issue at [6: 326], a duty specifically attached to ongoing existence of a particular people, rests on grounds other than the innate right of humanity as such.

14. Kant's only other published treatment of redistributive relief of the needy among a people occurs in the appendix, in a section titled "On the Right of the State Regarding *Perpetual* Foundations for Its Subjects." Kant there defends the right of the state to honor the spirit, rather than the letter, of the testator's will where better means have been discovered for carrying out the testator's intentions than those originally specified. Kant's example—giving the poor cash and thereby caring for them "better and more

cheaply" than by housing them in expensive institutions—values their independence, at least for Kant's immediate purposes, less as desirable in itself than as a more efficient means of "preserving" for the people what is theirs. [6: 367] The intrinsic value of giving the poor as much personal independence as possible is taken up below.

15. Sanchez also makes this point.

16. I here take issue with Ripstein's claim that this argument is improperly "instrumentalist": all state functions that are necessary to the execution of right, given our human condition as embodied rational beings, are "instrumentalist" in this sense.

17. Hence the appropriateness of the alternative proposed by Kant: exile to the provinces (within the state's territorial jurisdiction), a solution that would hardly suit were the main point of avoiding mass, albeit deserved, executions, that of sustaining a large and healthy home population.

18. See, for example, Ronald Beiner, "Paradoxes in Kant's Account of Citizenship," in *Kant and the Concept of Community*, ed. Chalton Payne and Lucas Thorp (Rochester, NY: University of Rochester Press, 2011).

19. On Kant's relation to Siéyès and the constitutional moderates, see also Reidar Maliks, *Kant's Politics in Context* (Oxford, UK: Oxford University Press, 2014).

20. According to Siéyès, "All inhabitants could enjoy in it the rights of *passive* citizens; all have the right to the protection of their person, of their property, of their liberty, etc. But all do not have the right to play an active role in the formation of public authorities; all are not *active* citizens. Women (at least at the present time), children, foreigners, and those others who contribute nothing to sustaining the public establishment should not be allowed to influence public life actively. Everyone is entitled to enjoy the advantages of society, but only those who contribute to the public establishment are true stockholders (*actionnaires*) of the great social enterprise. They alone are truly active citizens, true members of the association." Siéyès, 1789, 193–94.

21. When Kant's speaks of the innate right to "independence" from the elective wills of others, he uses "*Unabhängigkeit*," rather than "*Selbständigkeit*," a term he here exclusively reserves for citizenship in the "active" sense. (Cf., however, *Vorarbeiten* [19: 351]; and *Theory and Practice* [8: 295], where Kant equates *Selbstandigkeit* with being *sui iuris*.) To my knowledge, none of

the standard interpretations take note of the distinction between these two terms; indeed, most if not all treat them as equivalent—as reflected in the standard translation of both as "independence." I have here chosen to translate *Selbständigkeit*, more literally, as "self-subsistence," and Kant, indeed, here explicitly links the term with "substance" as distinguished from "inherence" (as the manner of existence of merely passive citizens).[6: 314] In *Theory and Practice*, Kant presents *sibisufficientia* as the Latin equivalent of *Selbständigkeit*. [8: 294] (In his 1891 translation of the Doctrine of Right, W. Hastie suggests "self-dependence.") Curiously, in *Perpetual Peace*, Kant replaces the formula "liberty, equality, self-subsistence," which figures both in *Theory and Practice* and in the *Rechtslehre*, with "freedom, dependence, and equality." [8: 349–50] On the meaning of *Selbständigkeit*, see the helpful treatment by C. Dierksmeier, "Kant on 'Selbständigkeit.'" Cf. the related *Ständigkeit*, meaning "constancy," "steadfastness," or "resolution." (The term *Selbständigkeit* later plays a major role in both Hegel's dialectic of master and slave, and in Heidegger's *Being and Time*.)

22. Cf. *Theory and Practice* [8: 290], which links the "civil condition" to the three principles of (1) the freedom of every member of society as a human being, (2) his equality with every other as a subject, and (3) the independence of each member of the commonwealth as a citizen; in *Toward Eternal Peace*, the civil condition is described, instead, in terms of (1) principles (*Prinzipien*) of freedom of the members of society as individuals, (2) principles (*Grundsätzen*) of the dependence (*Abhängigkeit*) of all on a common legislation as subjects; and (3) the law of their equality as citizens. [8: 349–50] In the *Metaphysics of Morals*, Kant includes all three principles as attributes of citizenship rather than merely independence (as in *Theory and Practice*) or lawful equality (as in *Toward Eternal Peace*); he also replaces "dependence," returning to the term for self-sufficiency or independence (*Selbständigkeit*) that he had used in *Theory and Practice* to describe the citizen tout court. That the more common German word for "independence" is *Unabhängigkeit* suggests that "self-sufficiency" or "self-subsistence" may be the more accurate translation, a suggestion further supported by the argument below. As to the significance of these changes, it must suffice here to note that Kant's restoration, in the *Rechtslehre*, of "self-sufficiency" to its former state of juridical importance is accompanied by an expansion of the concept of a citizen to include qualities previously reserved to members of

civil society as human beings and subjects. This newly integrative under-standing of the juridical personhood goes together with a new verbal link between the "essence" (*Wesen*) of the citizen and full-fledged participation in the common wealth (or, literally, the common essence) (*gemeinen Wesen*).

23. Kant's understanding of self-sufficiency thus not only falls outside Berlin's distinction between positive and negative freedom, but also is not to be identified with the "third concept of freedom" more recently champi-oned by Quentin Skinner. On Berlin's two concepts of freedom in relation to Kant, see also Williams, "Kant and Libertarianism."

24. That Kant only treats active and passive citizenship in this and the following *indented* paragraphs suggests that the entire discussion may be a concession to the empirical human condition rather than being nec-essary in a strictly a priori sense. [6: 205–6] Kant's stated intention at [6: 205–6] to use indentation in such contexts does not seem to have been carried out consistently enough to allow one to reach a firm con-clusion on this point.

25. Siéyès, *Arch Parl.*, August 27, 1789, tome VIII, p. 503. Ripstein's view, in this regard, is closer to Siéyès, according to the argument I am presenting here, than to Kant. Cf. Ripstein, *Force and Freedom*, 221. "Poverty, as Kant conceives it, is systematic: a person cannot use his or her own body, or even so much as occupy space, without the permission of another. The problem is not that some particular purpose depends on the choices of others, but that the pursuit of any purpose does. If all purposiveness depends on the grace of others, the dependent person is in the juridical position of a slave or serf." On my reading, by way of contrast, no one, even in the direst poverty, is entirely without the capacity to act purposively, i.e., to use his or her faculties [*Vermögen*] as he or she deems "right and good" without "depending in this" on the *Willkür* of another. [6: 312] If one cannot move in space without the permission of another, one can at least think as one chooses. This may seem a very limited sort of action, and indeed it is, but the conceptual point remains valid.

26. Kant equates being one's own master with being an active citizen in *Theory and Practice*, but not in the *Doctrine of Right*, which I am treating as the more definitive argument.

27. So conceived, this subsidiary law-giving authority represents one of the three *Gewalten* (along with the executive commander and the courts)

included in the "concept" of the state. The people play another active role: namely serving on juries—a demand, on Kant's part, wholly at odds with current Prussian practice. Trial by jury, long customary in England, was also adopted the French Constitution of 1793.

28. A "person" is a subject "whose actions may be imputed to him." "Moral personality" is the freedom of a rational being under moral laws, from which it follows, Kant says, that "a person is subject to no laws other than those he gives himself (either alone or at least along with others)." [6: 223] By the former sort of lawgiving, Kant would seem to have in mind internal legislation, by the latter (i.e., lawgiving along with others), he would seem to have in mind lawgiving through a general will, which binds externally even if internal (moral) self-legislation is lacking. Somewhat puzzlingly, Kant also treats condemned criminals as lacking in "civil" personality. [cf. Merle] There is, however, this crucial difference: unlike passive citizens, in whom civil personality lies, as it were, dormant and ready to actualize as will and opportunity permit, condemned criminals have themselves actively "forfeited" their civil personality by their own deed; in keeping with this decisive loss, they may be used by the state in any way, including being put to death, that does not make humanity itself into "something abominable" (e.g., no torture). [6: 331–33]

29. The peculiar case of women, about whose status Kant appears to vacillate, cannot be here addressed, for reasons of space. For a fuller treatment, see Susan Meld Shell, *Kant and the Limits of Autonomy* (Cambridge, MA: Harvard University Press, 2009).

30. That is, who have not willfully made poverty a "means of acquisition." Kant's own striking example of such no-fault neediness is that of abandoned children, whom the state is to charge the people "with not allowing to perish knowingly." [6: 326–27]

31. See, for example, Philip Pettit, *A Theory of Freedom* (Oxford, UK: Oxford University Press, 2001); and Quentin Skinner, *Liberty Before Liberalism* (Cambridge, UK: Cambridge University Press, 1998).

32. An additional, heretofore largely unexplored source for Kant's economic model here might be the exchange economy of self-subsistent artisans as outlined in Book Three of Rousseau's *Emile* (albeit with suitable changes in the direction of permitting an ever-growing expansion of the "means" available to society at large).

33. To be sure, independence in this sense (which I here translate as self-subsistence) *does* have civic relevance, but *not* for defining the bare minimum entailed by innate right as such. (I am indebted to Robert Taylor on this point.)

34. That wealth and active citizenship are not identical categories can be illustrated by the example of wealthy minors, whose funds are administered by others.

35. See note 10.

36. In the *Anthropology* and *Lectures on Pedagogy*, Kant suggests that the "idea of education" has not yet been fully worked out and, indeed, may never be.

37. See Abraham Lincoln. "Address to the Wisconsin State Agricultural Society," September 30, 1859.

Edmund Burke's Economics of Flourishing

YUVAL LEVIN
Ethics and Public Policy Center

The deep links between human flourishing and economic liberty are both vitally important and terribly underappreciated. Under the influence of modern economics, we too often now fall into viewing the economy as a kind of machine to be managed by technicians. This leads us to ignore the central place of economics in the human experience; to overlook its moral, social, and political character; and therefore to lose sight of its philosophical roots. In the process, we neglect the moral preconditions for the market economy, as well as some of the foremost moral and practical problems it poses for us.

Considering the link between economic liberty and human flourishing through the lens of the thought of Edmund Burke is a good way to be reminded of the moral and political depths of economic questions, because Burke thought about economics almost exclusively as a function of such deeper questions. He considered the "political economy" to be one coherent whole, and he thought about it in some ways that can inform our contemporary understanding. Such an exercise can be especially valuable for friends of free enterprise because Burke arrived by the end of his life at an argument for the market economy that we would find quite familiar, but which he reached by some much less familiar paths.

Burke was not an economist, of course, but more important he was a great critic of technical and technocratic ways of thinking about the lives of societies, and so his economic thought presents itself as a kind of critique of a lot of what now passes for economic thinking. The mechanistic understanding of the modern economy would be anathema to Burke. For him, economic life was best understood from the bottom up. He suggested that the power of markets, in our modern parlance, was that they enabled decisions to be made close to the ground and so aggregated society's knowledge in much the same way that our other core social institutions do.

Burke thus tended to think about economic relations in the way he thought about social relations—as something interpersonal that happens in those middle layers of society that were so important to him. That is still largely true, but it is not always true, and as we consider the relevance of Burke's economic thinking to our time, we should also reflect on what has changed and what that might mean.

The key to Burke's economics, as to much of the rest of his social and political thinking, was his belief in the incorrigible complexity of society. That belief was absolutely central to the arguments he made about both liberty and human flourishing and to his stout opposition, in what must strike us now as very modern terms, to government intervention in economic exchange. Let us, then, seek a sense of Burke's economics in his own terms.

⁓

At first glance, Burke's defense of the commercial society is a kind of tragic case. He recognizes the downsides and dark sides of the emerging market economy but argues that the alternatives would be worse, even (or especially) for the people most disadvantaged in commercial societies.

In *Reflections on the Revolution in France*, when he takes up the economic complaints of the revolutionaries and of their supporters in Britain, Burke takes note of "the innumerable servile, degrading, unseemly, unmanly, and often most unwholesome and pestiferous occupations, to which by the social economy so many wretches are inevitably doomed."[1] He can see why the conditions of so many workers would lead some observers to demand radical change. But he argues that the costs of remedying their situations by the sorts of extreme economic measures that the French would adopt—the costs not only to society as a whole but even to the particular wretches involved—would be far worse than their current suffering.

Unlike his acquaintance Adam Smith, Burke generally does not make a case for economic freedom as a transformative force that could dramatically improve the living conditions of the poor. He tends to emphasize the dangers of intervention and the harms of mercantilism more than the benefits and advantages of laissez-faire.

But I say this is so only at first glance because Burke's arguments about economics were actually rather minor elements of a larger argument about liberty and about human flourishing. Understood in that larger context, his essentially Smithian economic conclusions turn out to be rooted in more than a tragic acknowledgment of the absence of superior alternatives. We can reach Burke's view of human flourishing through his understanding of liberty and then look again at his explicitly economic arguments to see where they fit in.

Burke had a lot to say about liberty, but he was certainly not what we might today call a libertarian. In fact, he was moved to articulate his vision of human liberty precisely in opposition to a highly individualist, choice-centered understanding of what freedom entails and enables.

We might see that most clearly in one of Burke's lesser-known writings about the French Revolution. In early 1789, he received a letter from a young Frenchman named Charles-Jean-Francois DePont, whom he had met in London the year before. DePont would later be the formal addressee of *Reflections on the Revolution in France*, which was published as though it were a letter to him from Burke. But this actual exchange of letters between the two men happened before Burke had made any public statements about the revolution, and so before his views were known. DePont had clearly expected praise for the French when he asked for Burke's views, and an affirmative answer to his question about whether the revolution seemed to Burke to be an example of liberty in action.

What he actually received, of course, was decidedly not an affirmative answer. The French surely deserve liberty, Burke wrote in his letter to DePont, but they have mistaken the meaning of the term. True liberty "is not solitary, unconnected, individual, selfish liberty, as if every man was to regulate the whole of his conduct by his own will. The liberty I mean is social freedom. It is that state of things in which liberty is assured by the equality of restraint. . . . This kind of liberty is indeed but another name for justice; ascertained by wise laws, and secured by well-constructed institutions."[2]

Burke suggests in these remarks that radical individualism is the opposite of justice, and in that sense the opposite also of genuine liberty, and argues that freedom is a function of social relations and is obtained by equal self-restraint in a successful regime. His phrase "social freedom" is intended as a kind of counterpart to "individual liberty," a term much favored by the revolutionaries. And he argues that such social freedom or liberty properly understood, is the deepest source of Britain's strength.

Self-restraint is, as he says, at the core of this idea of liberty. He put the point even more forcefully in *Reflections* the following year:

> Men are qualified for civil liberty in exact proportion to their disposition to put moral chains upon their own appetites. In proportion as their love to justice is above their rapacity, in proportion as their soundness and sobriety of understanding is above their vanity and presumption, in proportion as they are more disposed to listen to the counsels of the wise and good, in preference to the flattery of knaves. Society cannot exist, unless a controlling power upon will and appetite be placed somewhere; and the less of it there is within, the more there must be without. It is ordained in the eternal constitution of things, that men of intemperate minds cannot be free. Their passions forge their fetters.[3]

This is an idea of liberty that is deeply intertwined with a particular notion of human flourishing. It is flourishing as a liberation from blinding passion and appetite—a freedom not only from outside constraint but also from an inner anarchy. And that kind of freedom is achieved in society, with the help of its institutions of moral formation.

At the heart of this vision of flourishing is therefore a sense of the interconnectedness of society—the way in which every human being is ensconced in a dense web of relationships that give society its shape and strength. Liberty is not a gift of society—it is the right of every person. But it is a right that can be exercised only within society and that requires immensely complicated social and political arrangements for its exercise and its perpetuation.

A year after publishing *Reflections*, and in response to some of its critics, Burke offered his most explicit articulation of this vision of society. In a pamphlet entitled *An Appeal from the New to the Old Whigs*, he makes it clear that his social vision begins precisely from the fact that we are born into a preexisting set of institutions and relationships:

> Dark and inscrutable are the ways by which we come into the world. The instincts which give rise to this mysterious process of nature are not of our making. But out of physical causes, unknown to us, per-haps unknowable, arise moral duties, which, as we are able perfectly to comprehend, we are bound indispensably to perform. Parents may not be consenting to their moral relation; but consenting or not, they are bound to a long train of burthensome duties towards those with whom they have never made a convention of any sort. Children are not consenting to their relation, but their relation, without their actual consent, binds them to its duties; or rather it implies their consent because the presumed consent of every rational creature is in unison with the predisposed order of things. Men come in that man-ner into a community with the social state of their parents, endowed with all the benefits, loaded with all the duties of their situation. If the social ties and ligaments, spun out of those physical relations which are the elements of the commonwealth, in most cases begin, and always continue, independently of our will, so without any stip-ulation, on our part, are we bound by that relation called our country, which comprehends (as it has been well said) "all the charities of all." Nor are we left without powerful instincts to make this duty as dear and grateful to us, as it is awful and coercive.[4]

Each human being arrives in the world as a new member of an old order, and far from a constraint upon our freedom that must be overcome, this fact is what makes our freedom possible. The primary reason for that, Burke argues, is that human beings have to be *formed* for freedom and are not born with that form. It is a social achievement. Social theories that begin with the free and rational individual alone seemed to him to beg a question they can never answer: where does this free person come from? Every person, after all, comes from a family—which is not a liberal institution—and enters the world both unable to exercise freedom and encumbered by all kinds of social relations that operate as restraints. To get from that beginning to the exercise of liberty, let alone to a society of free people exercising their liberty, requires much more than the absence of restraint.

It requires a social order, a political order, an economic order, and a moral order. The only genuine liberty, Burke argued in 1774, "is a liberty connected with order: that not only exists along with order and virtue but that cannot exist at all without them. It inheres in good and steady government, as in its substance and vital principle."[5]

Human flourishing, in this sense, is possible only in a rich and complex social order adapted to enable it. And that adaptation is key for Burke. A free society is not found at the end of a syllogism or on the right side of an equation. It is a matter of gradual evolution, a long-term trial and error process. Society's institutions are means of learning how to enable flourishing and happiness.

That is the case, Burke argues, not because there are no principles of justice or natural law that should guide society but because we cannot access those principles as directly as we would like. We cannot generally access them directly through the sort of rational science of politics that the enlightenment promised, nor can we do so through the natural-law arguments of the church. We generally cannot know them directly at all. But we can come to know them indirectly through the experience of social and political life itself. The institutions of our society are always seeking them out, and the shapes those institutions take are a function of that process of seeking.

The historical experience of social and political life for Burke consists in essence of a kind of rubbing up against the principles of natural justice, and the institutions and practices that survive that experience—that are found by men and women across generations to provide them with flourishing and happy lives—take on something of the shape of those principles, because only those that have that shape do survive that process. So over time, provided they develop through continuous, incremental change at the margins rather than sharp breaks and jostles, societies come to express in their institutions, charters, traditions, and habits a kind of simulacrum of the standard of justice. Society as it exists after such long experience comes to offer an approximation of society as it should exist.

This is the essence of Burke's conservatism. It is rooted in a profound epistemological modesty and involves a rejection of highly technical ways of thinking about social life and social change and an emphasis on evolved institutions that stand between the individual and the nation as a whole and channel dispersed social knowledge (as opposed to engineered institutions that stand above it all and apply centralized technical knowledge). Those kinds of social institutions, and that mode of social change, make possible the balance of order and freedom that allows for genuine human liberty, and therefore for human flourishing.

⧉

With that in mind, we can more fully appreciate Burke's economics. Burke's tragic view of the benefits of capitalism is fundamentally a rejection of the alternatives, which even in his time involved technocratic attempts to manage social relations in ways that seemed to him likely only to undermine the potential for human flourishing. But in that rejection is also an affirmation of an alternative understanding of human flourishing—an alternative to technocratic liberalism.

We can see this most clearly in Burke's most extended discussion of economics. In the last years of his life, Burke became deeply involved in a debate about a proposal in Parliament to manage the wages of farm workers—essentially a minimum wage for agricultural laborers. He was a staunch opponent of the idea, and he put his reasons in writing in the form of a kind of memo to Prime Minister William Pitt, which was published shortly after his death as "Thoughts and Details on Scarcity."

Burke opens his case with a statement of his general outlook on the subject:

> To provide for us in our necessities is not in the power of Government. It would be a vain presumption in statesmen to think they can do it. The people maintain them, and not they the people. It is in the power of Government to prevent much evil; it can do very little positive good in this, or perhaps in any thing else.[6]

He goes on to argue that the proposed legislation is premised on the notion that a contract between an employer and an employee involves the former abusing the latter, but that in fact the nature of contracts involves finding an arrangement that reconciles different interests. "In the case of the farmer and the labourer, their interests are always the same, and it is absolutely impossible that their free contracts can be onerous to either party."[7] He then frames potential objections to this view in a most ungenerous light:

> I shall be told by the zealots of the sect of regulation that this may be true, and may be safely committed to the convention of the farmer and the labourer, when the latter is in the prime of his youth, and at the time of his health and vigour, and in ordinary times of abundance. But in calamitous seasons, under accidental illness, in declining life, and with the pressure of a numerous offspring, the future nourishers of the community but the present drains and blood-suckers of those who produce them, what is to be done?[8]

But this argument, too, he says, fails to take account of the nature of economic relationships:

> And, first, I premise that labour is, as I have already intimated, a commodity, and as such, an article of trade. If I am right in this notion, then labour must be subject to all the laws and principles of trade, and not to regulations foreign to them, and that may be totally inconsistent with those principles and those laws. When any commodity is carried to market, it is not the necessity of the vender, but the

necessity of the purchaser that raises the price. The extreme want of the seller has rather (by the nature of things with which we shall in vain contend) the direct contrary operation. If the goods at market are beyond the demand, they fall in their value; if below it, they rise. The impossibility of the subsistence of a man, who carries his labour to a market, is totally beside the question in this way of viewing it. The only question is, what is it worth to the buyer? But if authority comes in and forces the buyer to a price, who is this in the case (say) of a farmer, who buys the labour of ten or twelve labouring men, and three or four handycrafts, what is it, but to make an arbitrary division of his property among them?[9]

Such jerks of authority, Burke suggests, are generally well-intentioned—driven by a desire to equalize unequal conditions. But the nature of a free economy means that such egalitarianism frequently has disastrous consequences:

A perfect equality will indeed be produced; that is to say, equal want, equal wretchedness, equal beggary, and on the part of the partitioners, a woeful, helpless, and desperate disappointment. Such is the event of all compulsory equalizations. They pull down what is above. They never raise what is below: and they depress high and low together beneath the level of what was originally the lowest.[10]

And the notion that the agricultural economy should be treated differently than commerce in the cities is equally ignorant of basic economic principles, Burke argues:

A greater and more ruinous mistake cannot be fallen into, than that the trades of agriculture and grazing can be conducted upon any other than the common principles of commerce; namely, that the producer should be permitted, and even expected, to look to all possible profit which, without fraud or violence, he can make; to turn plenty or scarcity to the best advantage he can; to keep back or to bring forward his commodities at his pleasure; to account to no one for his stock or for his gain. On any other terms he is the slave

of the consumer; and that he should be so is of no benefit to the
consumer. No slave was ever so beneficial to the master as a free-
man that deals with him on an equal footing by convention, formed
on the rules and principles of contending interests and compro-
mised advantages.[11]

The same is true of the people who stand between the farmer and
the market:

What is true of the farmer is equally true of the middle man; whether
the middle man acts as factor, jobber, salesman, or speculator, in the
markets of grain. These traders are to be left to their free course; and
the more they make, and the richer they are, and the more largely they
deal, the better both for the farmer and consumer, between whom
they form a natural and most useful link of connection; though, by
the machinations of the old evil counsellor, Envy, they are hated and
maligned by both parties.[12]

Indeed, Burke turns out to be immensely impressed by the power
of markets to apply knowledge that their would-be regulators could
never possess:

The balance between consumption and production makes price. The
market settles, and alone can settle, that price. Market is the meeting
and conference of the consumer and producer, when they mutually
discover each other's wants. Nobody, I believe, has observed with any
reflection what market is, without being astonished at the truth, the
correctness, the celerity, the general equity, with which the balance of
wants is settled. They who wish the destruction of that balance, and
would fain by arbitrary regulation decree, that defective production
should not be compensated by encreased price, directly lay their axe
to the root of production itself.[13]

Burke concludes with a general statement about the proper
relation between government and the economy. "My opinion," he
writes, "is against an over-doing of any sort of administration, and

more especially against this most momentous of all meddling on the part of authority; the meddling with the subsistence of the people."[14]

⋙

This Burkean case for a free economy as an essential component of a genuinely free society is rooted in a view of human flourishing that emphasizes the moral preconditions for freedom in a complex, layered society. It proceeds from a profound epistemic humility. And it advances a model of gradual, incremental change through bottom-up trial and error at the margins.

It understands the system of economic liberty as an embodiment of a traditionalist view of society, and therefore as itself a kind of precondition for human flourishing. But its commitment to the market economy is not dogmatic or absolute but prudent and practical, and subservient to a commitment to the genuine liberty of virtuous citizens.

It is also, I would hasten to say, the product of observing the emergence of a commercial society in Britain but not yet of the emergence of the industrial economy, with its mass scale and its immense transformative, even revolutionary, social consequences. Burke's capitalism is an inextricable element of his fundamentally social conservatism, but it is so in part because he did not expect the market economy to overturn the social order. He saw it, rather, as an embodiment of the social order, and he viewed those who would seek to regulate and manage the economy as disrupting stable social arrangements.

In the subsequent centuries, things did not quite turn out that way. The market economy has in fact turned out to be a profoundly disruptive and revolutionary social force—overturning traditional arrangements in every realm of life, for good and bad. The advantages it has provided us are those that Burke had hoped it might: immense wealth and with it immense freedom. But the challenges it has posed for us are actually often those that Burke had thought it would prevent: social dislocation, insecurity, and breakdown.

While the route Burke took to his defense of the market economy is very instructive for us, therefore, especially because it gets near the root of his case for tradition as a means of change and adaptation, it does not make Burke simply a capitalist in our modern terms. He was a traditionalist and valued markets for their embodiment of a kind of humility and for their channeling of knowledge from the bottom up. That made him a friend of markets to the extent that they support and uphold the complex social order that enables human flourishing. They surely do so to a very great extent, but never perfectly. And it is precisely the friends of markets who should be most willing to acknowledge that, and to seek for ways to address it that themselves partake of humility about human knowledge and power, for the sake of liberty and human flourishing.

Notes

1. Edmund Burke, *The Writings and Speeches of Edmund Burke*, ed. Paul Langford (Oxford: Oxford University Press, 2000), VIII, 209.

2. Edmund Burke, *The Correspondence of Edmund Burke*, ed. Thomas Copeland (Chicago: University of Chicago Press, 1978), VI, 42.

3. Burke, *Writings*, VIII, 332.

4. Edmund Burke, *Further Reflections on the Revolution in France*, ed. Daniel Ritchie (Indianapolis, IN: Liberty Fund, 1992), 161.

5. Burke, *Writings*, III, 59.

6. Ibid., IX, 120.

7. Ibid., 124.

8. Ibid., 126.

9. Ibid.

10. Ibid., 127.

11. Ibid., 130.

12. Ibid., 132.

13. Ibid., 133.

14. Ibid., 145.

Capitalism as a Road to Serfdom?
Tocqueville on Economic Liberty
and Human Flourishing

STEVEN BILAKOVICS

University of California, Los Angeles

Of Alexis de Tocqueville's many deserved claims to renown, his penetrating, prescient critique of socialism surely ranks right at the top. The prospect of socialism is so troubling to Tocqueville for two main reasons. First, the promise of socialism is pitched at precisely the level to entice the peoples of democratic modernity. Given the desires, values, and self-image of the modern human being—the being who has lost faith in aristocracy and believes in the self-evidence of equality—the socialist utopia may prove too seductive to resist. Second, for Tocqueville socialism constitutes the primary threat to—the very antithesis of—human flourishing. The dispirited souls of socialism would be incapable of perceiving, much less acting on, the freedom, responsibility, and dignity unique to the human condition.

So how does Tocqueville understand human flourishing? In his view, the good life—the fully human life, characterized by the excellences and happiness appropriate to the human being—is the life of liberty. Without getting too far lost in the labyrinth of meanings Tocqueville ascribes to liberty, we can sketch out two basic notions he develops: the first he views as proper to the common man of democratic times, and the second is characteristic of the superior element of any age. We can call these, respectively, the liberty of the good citizen and the liberty of the noble personality.

The liberty of the citizen is comprised in no small part of the formal rights of conscience, speech, association, and property. But for Tocqueville these civil liberties—the right to be left alone, in the silence of the laws, within a legal framework that secures property and persons—are at most half the picture. At least as important is political liberty—political participation and the use of one's civil liberties in the exercise of political power—inscribed within a culture of robust political participation that reinforces the experience of real self-government. To enjoy the privacy rights—the "negative liberties"—of non-interference absent the opportunity, developed capacity, and habituated disposition for political association and action is to in effect suffer the experience of being free but powerless. For all of his newfound rights and liberties, the modern, apolitical individual can see and aspire only so far as to be "the king of his own castle." This is why, beyond the public life of voluntary associations in civil society—whether bowling leagues or mass interest groups—the specifically *political* public life of participation in local self-government is paramount for Tocqueville. In modern times, what Tocqueville calls the "art of freedom" is the "art of association"—and of political association in particular. Everyday political associations constitute the infrastructure of the good society and the good life for the citizens of democracy. It is where the individual becomes a citizen—achieves the station of citizen—by moderating *and* elevating his view out of narrow, unfettered partiality and developing his capacity for practical judgment through collective deliberation over practical political issues. Through political association the citizen at once exercises power and learns prudence. Thus for Tocqueville, we can say that liberty is realized through political public activity, just as for Aristotle virtue is realized through the practice of politics.

Tocqueville's second notion of liberty—that of the noble personality—subsumes but transcends the liberty of the good citizen. This liberty too implies a capacity for action, but one born of the virile force of one's inner resources rather than through the cooperation of the many. It is an aristocratic rather than a democratic liberty. In democratic times it takes shape in the romantic heroism of the principled, spirited, and above all passionate few. Where the exercise of good citizenship is driven by what Tocqueville calls "self-interest well understood"—the enlightened recognition that one's own good is always bound up with and contingent on the common good—this second notion of liberty follows upon immoderate self-transcendence and reckless self-sacrifice. Where Tocqueville found the liberty of the citizen in the energetic bustle and noise of American public life (at least in the North), he depicts the liberty of the noble soul as in full bloom in France, among the revolutionary "men of '89"—those who in a grand, sublime, tragic act of imagination attempted to remake the world in the name of the rights of man.

Socialism signifies the abolition of liberty in both of these iterations. In a famous debate before the Constituent Assembly in France on September 12, 1848, Tocqueville argued that "socialism stands for the community of property, the right to be provided with work, absolute equality, State control of all activities of individuals, despotic legislation, and the total submerging of each citizen's personality in the group mind." In a now-familiar argument that he pioneered, Tocqueville analyzes the advance of socialism in terms of the creep of "administrative centralization"—what Max Weber would later describe as the rationalization and bureaucratization of human life. Here, power concentrates in the organs of the state, and the state projects this power to plan, oversee, and regulate most every sphere of human activity. All the world is, in turn, represented as a system, a mechanical organization of complex but quantifiable materials and forces, which operates, if properly managed, predictably and efficiently according to design. Indeed, once we think and talk in terms of "systems"—"the economic system," for instance—we are well down the road to centralization and managerial administration. Human culture is abstracted into a "society" of homogeneous, disconnected but interdependent individuals. Human action is channeled into a productive workforce. Human judgment becomes, in turns, a matter of professional or scientific expertise, utilitarian calculation, and unmoored speculation. And in the consequent empire of bureaucracy, individual initiative and the human spirit whither. A totalizing network of uniform rules and regulations enables the centralized administration of the demographied nation and simultaneously suffocates personal responsibility and self-government.

The prospect of socialism is all the more troubling, in Tocqueville's eyes, because its promise is so tempting to modern democratic peoples. In the egalitarian mass of anonymous mediocrity, where the experience of individual insignificance—of being "lost in the crowd," as Tocqueville often writes, of innumerable similar others—is all but inevitable, we the people abdicate our newfound sovereignty, forsake our rights and responsibilities, and invite our own superintendence. The individual comes to feel powerless, unable not only to make a difference in the world but moreover to influence or even understand the societal tides that buffet his own existence. Adrift and submerged, he casts off all things demanding or higher and turns his attention toward his own most immediate material needs and desires. The inhabitants of democratic society end up in the terrible position of being wholly self-centered without the resources for self-respect. In their "excessive humility," as Tocqueville puts it, such a prostrate, infantilized people fall happily into the arms of the paternal (or better, maternal) state—the vast, impersonal power that relieves people of the burdens of thinking or acting for themselves and promises to take care of them. The outcome is the soul's degradation and the spirit's enervation. Along these lines, socialism strikes at the very roots of human pride and dignity, culminating in no less than a brave new world dystopia of humanity domesticated.

Tocqueville sketches this portrait of centralization, regulation, and servility most indelibly toward the end of *Democracy in America*, where he offers his vision of the rise of an "immense tutelary power" and its "mild despotism." In a chapter entitled "What Kind of Despotism Democratic Nations Have to Fear," Tocqueville writes,

I am trying to imagine what new features despotism might have in today's world: I see an innumerable host of men, all alike and equal, endlessly hastening after petty and vulgar pleasures with which they fill their souls. Each of them drawn into himself, is virtually a stranger to the fate of all the others. . . .

Over these men stands an immense tutelary power, which assumes sole responsibility for securing their pleasure and watching over their fate. It is absolute, meticulous, regular, provident, and mild. It would resemble paternal authority if only its purpose were the same, namely, to prepare men for manhood. But on the contrary, it seeks only to keep them in childhood irrevocably. It likes citizens to rejoice, provided they think only of rejoicing. . . . It provides for their security, foresees and takes care of their needs, facilitates their pleasures, manages their most important affairs, directs their industry, regulates their successions, and divides their inheritances. . . .

Equality paved the way for all these things by preparing men to put up with them and even look upon them as a boon.

The sovereign, after taking individuals one by one in his powerful hands and kneading them to his liking, reaches out to embrace society as a whole. Over it he spreads a fine mesh of uniform, minute, and complex rules, through which not even the most original minds and most vigorous souls can poke their heads above the crowd. He does not break men's wills but softens, bends, and guides them. He seldom forces anyone to act but consistently opposes action. . . . Rather than tyrannize, he inhibits, represses, saps, stifles, and stultifies, and in the end he reduces each nation to nothing but a flock of timid and industrious animals, with the government as its shepherd.[1]

This extraordinarily rich passage is surely the most famous and often quoted in Tocqueville's writings, and it has become the touchstone critique of Big Government, the "nanny" welfare state, and creeping socialism. F. A. Hayek, for instance, quotes this passage prominently and at length in *The Road to Serfdom* and notes that the title of his book is a reworded homage to Tocqueville's phrase "the road to servitude."

Against this image of centralization one might assume that Tocqueville would be the strongest of advocates for economic liberty and what would come to be called free-market capitalism. In a number of passages of *Democracy in America* Tocqueville does indeed celebrate the prudence, practicality, do-it-yourself attitude, and work-ethic virtues of the American businessman. He famously contrasts the vibrant energy of the free-labor North with the ethical lethargy of the slave-owning South. And he marvels at the reckless passions and chance-taking initiative of the American entrepreneur, who seems to love the gamble more than the gain. There is a sort of honor and even heroism to be found in the American trader, Tocqueville writes, who risks his life on the wild frontier or the open ocean in his incalculable passion to make a few pennies more than his competitor. The American applies the maxims of war to business, and he finds great pride in his commercial ventures and conquests.

But for Tocqueville this is only part of the picture of the rising bourgeois way of life. As with most multidimensional phenomena—above all the rise of democratic modernity itself—Tocqueville is deeply ambivalent about the new socio-economy. There is an underside to every appearance, and an underside to the underside. Even as he admires the business-minded American, he expresses nothing but contempt in his private correspondence for "the little bourgeois pot of soup" of his native French politics and society—the shameless, spineless class that serially courted Napoleonic despotism. He writes in *Democracy* of his concern that industrialization may give rise to a new, cruel, and exploitative faux-aristocracy comprised of the owners of the means of production, alongside a debased, stultified, cog-in-the-assembly-line working class. Ultimately, he worries that the bourgeois ethos of commercial society may exacerbate the worst pathologies of democratic modernity—its vulgar materialism and dissociative individualism—thereby paving the way for administrative centralization, socialism, and mild despotism. Capitalism itself may be a road to serfdom.

In this context, let's look at four elements of economic liberty: private property rights, freedom of contract, free enterprise, and the free market. In Tocqueville's view, property rights are an essential component of liberty and check upon government expansion. Property ownership—and landownership in particular—serve to decentralize power and buttress the independence and sense of self-worth of the individual, introducing a semblance of the aristocratic disposition into democratic times. Moreover, private property and the sense that one has something to lose generate a conservative ethic that counterbalances the revolutionary flights of innovation to which democratic peoples are prone.

At the same time, widespread property ownership and the pre-occupation with material wealth may make a people excessively conservative, even to the point of illiberality. Afraid to lose what they have, people may come to value the stability of the established order above all. The security of the self and its possessions may become paramount. Such peoples would fear anarchy more than tyranny, and popular unrest more than authoritarianism. They would be peaceful and tranquil, orderly and mild, like a flock of timid and industrious animals. Further, the passion for acquisition may give way to an imbecilic *need* for material well-being—for comfort and pleasure in addition to security—and an idiotic privatism that saps the civic and manly virtues and blinds citizens to the very preconditions of their well-being. Consumed by the desires of the body, the individual comes to neglect the public good and the goods of the soul. Ambition becomes constant and pressing but petty, happiness translates to pleasure, and flourishing reduces to success at getting whatever one desires. When "commercial mores" come to reign, constant superficial flux and motion will mask a deep, dispirited inertia, and great revolutions (first political, then intellectual) will become rare in a sort of stagnant, bourgeois end of history.

"When I see . . . love of property [become] so restless and ardent" and "citizens continue to confine themselves ever more narrowly within the sphere of petty domestic interests, . . . becoming all but invulnerable to those great and powerful public emotions that roil nations but also develop and renew them," Tocqueville writes, "I tremble, I confess, that they might eventually allow themselves to become so entranced by a contemptible love of present pleasures that their interest in their own future and the future of their offspring might disappear."

Tocqueville continues:

I am afraid [the new societies] will end up all too invariably attached to the same institutions, the same prejudices, and the same mores, so that the human race will stop progressing and narrow its horizons. I fear that . . . man will exhaust his energies in petty, solitary, and sterile changes, and that humanity, though constantly on the move, will cease to advance."[2]

As with property rights, freedom of contract is, in Tocqueville's view, a valuable check on government centralization and expansion. Moreover, it imbues the relationships between individuals with a sense of formal dignity and mutual respect. But the notion of the contracting individual as an autonomous chooser of his own goods and ends—his own way of life—may also inflame the obsessive, self-subverting pursuit of independence that Tocqueville calls individualism. Where self-interest well understood leads citizens to understand that, particularly in democratic times, they can only do well together, individualism is the erroneous judgment that I can stand alone—indeed that I must, in the name of freedom, sever myself from the influence, aid, and support of others. To be free, I must be self-sufficient and provide—financially, but also intellectually and spiritually—for myself. The aspiration to, and even routine expectation of, such radical independence leads ultimately to intellectual disorientation and spiritual exhaustion, and so to ever deeper and more ashamed forms of dependence. Citizens increasingly come to need the support from others that they ethically cannot accept. And so they seek out impersonal sources of patronage, dependence upon which will degrade to a lesser degree their egalitarian principles and self-conception.

The mistake here is again one of excess: that human beings can be, beyond self-governing, actually self-sufficient—the sovereign individual of liberal contract theory and the self-made man of capitalist fantasy. Tocqueville never pays much attention to social contract theory and its foundational image of atomistic individuals in a state of nature. The prepolitical, presocial, free-standing individual is, for Tocqueville, largely unimaginable and irrelevant to questions of human nature, justice, and rule. His political sociology refers rather to history. It is oriented by reflection upon the cultures and constitutions—the regime forms—from which the human being develops its particular intellectual and ethical character. His analysis of freedom and authority in human association focuses not on

voluntary consent but rather on the mores—the sociocultural prejudices—that frame a people's goods and ends. His concern is not the
formal legitimacy of contract theory, but rather the frameworks of
authority—both secular and transcendent—that orient and elevate
judgment. For Tocqueville, a free society coheres less around voluntarism—a preoccupation with which leads to an exclusive adoration
of the human will—than around the ingrained *habit* of voluntarism.

Indeed, many of the forms of association Tocqueville most fully
affirms—such as juries and townships—are not immediately constituted via contractual agreement or voluntary membership. Rather,
citizens are in a sense drafted and put into a company of those
among whom there is no particular shared interest. Unlike voluntary associations—professional associations, interest groups, and so
on—such institutions educate citizens by compelling them to consider the good from a less partial, common, and public perspective.

As we have seen, Tocqueville celebrates the free-enterprise economic (and political) activity characteristic of the American North.
Here too, though, the danger arises that economic vibrancy and
socioeconomic mobility may themselves worsen the individualism and materialism of modern democratic societies. The constant
hope of rising and fear of falling breeds an agitated restiveness in
the American way of life. Americans pursue ever more even as they
are unsure of their own purposes. Appetite becomes insatiable, and
desire endless. Progress comes to be defined in exclusively secular,
materialistic terms, which in turn produces a sort of moral nearsight-
edness and ethical anxiety. The body's mortality rather than the soul's
salvation comes to define human time, turning existence into a fever-
ish rush to nowhere. The spirit of competition undermines the habits of cooperation and association upon which a healthy democratic
society depends. Money, as the sole remaining medium of power,
influence, and efficacy for the vast majority of people, becomes of
far more than pecuniary importance. And the rewards of economic
life draw people away from politics and civic life. "It is not necessary," Tocqueville writes, "to do violence to such a people in order to
strip them of the rights they enjoy, they themselves willingly loosen
their hold. The discharge of political duties appears to them to be a

troublesome impediment which diverts them from their occupation and business."[3]

To speak of "the free market" in the context of Tocqueville's thought is a bit anachronistic, but he clearly rejects the centralized administration and regulation of any sphere of society, including that of economic activity. But he just as clearly questions the sort of Scottish Enlightenment vision of a self-regulating—spontaneous as opposed to planned—society that coheres primarily around the motive of self-interest, the division of labor, and free trade.

First, the free play of self-interest in commercial society would likely yield the lowest-common-denominator pursuit of material well-being. In the free market, the vulgar always costs less and sells more than things of virtue. Left to the guidance of the invisible hand, modern nations would move spontaneously toward consumerism, privatism, and mass-market uniformity. Thus is *Democracy in America* addressed precisely to the planners of society—not its bureaucrats but its statesmen and educators.

Second, the very idea of "the market"—wherein impersonal forces and immutable laws operate within an incomprehensibly complex and self-regulating system that provides for our wants and meets our needs—may well contribute to the sense of fatalism Tocqueville so fears. Above all, Tocqueville despises the degrading resignation born of a belief in determinism—whether rooted in the vast, overawing abstractions of history, genetic nature, society, or the bureaucratic state. If individuals come to view the market as natural or even sacrosanct, or to live in silent awe of market forces as one might before the forces of nature, the free market will end up as one more aspect of modern life that seems to steer the individual's fate beyond his understanding and without his say.

Third, while Tocqueville believes that human beings do have a natural desire and capacity for freedom, he argues that modern democratic peoples are prone to misunderstand political liberty's cultural and ethical preconditions—the habits of heart and mind that dispose citizens to embrace civic and political association along with the burdens of collective self-government. And they are prone to miscalculate freedom's necessary and proper limits in the pursuit of radical independence. In their egalitarian hostility to every sem-blance of external authority, democratic peoples develop an aversion to the very concepts of judgment, virtue, and education—all those concepts that take shape around hierarchies of higher and lower, superior and inferior, noble and base. "Freedom" thus becomes syn-onymous with choice (the liberty of conscience, for instance, reduces to the right to choose one's religion), but absent all frameworks of authority that orient and elevate one's choices and make something worth choosing, the result is choice without reason or judgment—simply the subjective expression of will.

Freedom, in turn, is taken to either licentious or transcendent excesses—freedom as debauchery or autonomy. The sole remaining ethical points of reference lie at the immoderate extremes of human potentiality—sovereign self-rule or the instant gratification of the desire for material well-being. The human being comes to imagine himself as paradoxically at once more and less than a political ani-mal. Recall Aristotle's reasoning that "the man who is isolated, who is unable to share in the benefits of political association, or has no need to share because he is already self-sufficient, in no part of the city, and must therefore be either a beast or a god."[4] In his newfound freedom, democratic man considers himself both beast *and* god.

Tocqueville concludes that the realization of the freedom prom-ised by the rise of democracy cannot be spontaneous, the product of a laissez-faire absence or the silence of the laws. Freedom becomes an art—not something natural but rather to be learned and practiced—precisely because political association has become an art. At bottom Tocqueville is closer to Aristotle than Adam Smith in his view of liberty and human flourishing, looking less to the invisible hand of free-market society than to the deliberative practices of political society.

Ultimately, Tocqueville remains too much of a small "r" republi-can to wholeheartedly embrace the economic liberty of commercial society. He is too aware of the corrupting influence of luxury, the corrosive effects of privatism, and so on. Hayek, and following him Milton Friedman, argue that political liberty cannot be preserved in the absence of economic liberty. Tocqueville would agree. But for

Tocqueville our situation is never so simple, and there is always an underside to the values by which we live. Economic liberty is essential to political freedom, but also a threat to political liberty. For Tocqueville, sustaining the culture of political participation, and therefore of political liberty, is paramount. Political liberty (along with the authority of religion) provides something of a remedy to the pathologies of the modern democratic way of life—its individualism and materialism, its logical and psychological corollaries that subvert every source of noble pride and dignity, the dispiriting experience of being free but powerless. Insofar as economic liberty reinforces political liberty and the mores of self-government, it is of great value. Insofar as the elements of commercial society and free-market capitalism are affirmed to immoderate extremes—and particularly insofar as they produce the depoliticization of self and society—they should be criticized and checked.

Ayn Rand famously claimed that she was for the separation of economics and state for the same reasons that most are for the separation of church and state. For Tocqueville, the more significant remedy to Big Government centralization and the urge to welfare maternalism—and the real recipe for the good life and the good society in democratic times—is less the separation of economics and state than the separation of politics and state. The key to human flouring is less economic liberty than political liberty, and its venue less the unfettered free market than a culture of vital political association and activity.

Notes

1. Alexis de Tocqueville, *Democracy in America*, trans. Arthur Goldhammer (New York: Library of America, 2004), vol. 2, part 4, chap. 6.

2. Ibid., 2.3.21

3. Ibid.

4. Aristotle, *Politics*, 1.1253a25.

John Stuart Mill on Economic Liberty and Human Flourishing

RICHARD BOYD
Georgetown University

There would seem to be few reasons to dispute John Stuart Mill's (1806–73) classical liberal credentials. Mill's celebrated 1859 treatise *On Liberty* is a paean to virtually unlimited liberty of speech, religious belief, opinion, and expression. There Mill famously makes the case that individuals should enjoy perfect liberty to act so long as their actions do not pose a direct and proximate harm to others. Mill extols individuality and defends a vision of history in which the iconoclastic and eccentric ideas of one age fuel moral development and material progress. Moving beyond his moral philosophy, Mill's influential work in political economy likewise conveys a strong sense of his liberalism—if not libertarianism. Although his position drifts through successive editions, the monumental *Principles of Political Economy* (1848) stands as one of the most influential 19th-century affirmations of laissez-faire, free trade, and economic liberalization.

Mill's place in the pantheon of philosophical liberals has been acknowledged, albeit with some hesitation, by many interpreters, but not everyone has found him to be such a dyed-in-the-wool defender of economic liberty.[1] No less discerning a student of Mill's life and corpus than F. A. Hayek intuited a strand of what he called "constructivist rationalism" that threatened to carry Mill's later political thought in the direction of socialism rather than classical liberalism.[2] Some of Mill's more immediate legatees on the left such as L. T. Hobhouse and Harold Laski regarded Mill as a transitional figure between old and new English liberalisms.[3] Mill's collectivistic affinities have been discernible since the 19th century, but the full-blown case for Mill as an advocate of "social control" reemerged with Joseph Hamburger's controversial book *J. S. Mill on Liberty and Control* (2000), which characterized Mill as enamored of efforts to regulate and steer human conduct.[4]

Without denying that Mill's arguments have proved useful for classical liberalism and a defense of limited government—or that Mill is indeed a liberal "of sorts"—the following chapter is meant to tease out aspects of Mill's social and political philosophy about which defenders of economic liberty ought to feel at least some trepidation. My comments echo traditional criticisms of Mill as a harbinger of collectivism, but the features identified here also differ from those elements of Mill's thought that raised the hackles of Hayek and Mises—or elicited the praise of the Fabian socialists, Hobhouse, Laski, and others on the left.[5]

Any analysis of Mill is complicated by his uneasy synthesis of so many discrepant influences—ranging from the romanticism of Wilhelm von Humboldt or Samuel Taylor Coleridge to the rationalism of Jeremy Bentham to the sociological positivism of August Comte to the chastened aristocratic sensibilities of Alexis de Tocqueville. The sum of all this, I argue, is that Mill's political thought breaks in fundamental ways from the natural rights philosophy or "classical liberalism" of the 17th and 18th centuries. By disavowing natural rights in favor of a peculiar species of utilitarianism, Millian liberalism ends up being compossible with various forms of social control. Moreover, and with respect to this volume's broader thematic question of human flourishing and the good life, Mill seems to be very far from reckoning a life of trade as conducive to those refined sensibilities and higher pleasures he places at the epicenter of moral progress and human development. At minimum, for Mill, commerce is a necessary means for unleashing the material civilization upon which moral progress rests. At maximum, as we will see, he regards commercial society as an impediment to the cultivation of moral discernment, character, and rugged individuality.

From Nature to Utility: On the Utilitarian Foundations of Millian Liberalism

Taking Mill at his own word, it seems self-evident that he was at least some kind of "liberal." Indeed he is arguably more deserving of this appellation than John Locke, Thomas Jefferson, James Madison, or other "classical liberals" for whom the term "liberal" is anachronistic. In the *Autobiography* and elsewhere, Mill identifies with the cause of Benthamite Reform—the 19th-century political movement and ideology from which we derive the contemporary appellation "liberalism." Speaking of the early period of Radicalism, when "Liberalism seemed to be becoming the tone of the time," Mill counts himself as among the "most active of its small number."[6]

Notwithstanding his self-identification, there is at least one indisputable difference between Mill's species of liberalism and that of his 17th- and 18th-century predecessors: namely, his utilitarian repudiation of natural rights. Classical liberals such as Locke and Jefferson maintained that liberty is grounded in certain laws of nature, if not the divine will of God, and consequently that human beings were endowed with absolute and inviolable natural rights. For his part, Mill follows in the footsteps of his mentor Jeremy Bentham, who famously dismissed the notion of natural rights as "nonsense upon stilts."[7] Instead of a universal, metaphysical entailment of pre-political natural laws, rights are artifacts of particular laws and political institutions. As such, for Bentham and Mill, they are susceptible to being either extended by degree or potentially withheld depending on whether they contribute to the overall utility of society.

Maybe the most revealing passage in all of *On Liberty* is Mill's utilitarian disclaimer in Chapter 1:

> It is proper to state that I forgo any advantage which could be derived to my argument [for liberty] from the idea of abstract right as a thing independent of utility. I regard utility as the ultimate appeal on all ethical questions; but it must be utility in the largest sense, grounded on the permanent interests of man as a progressive being.[8]

This précis of Mill's philosophy is telling for several reasons. First, while Mill doesn't here categorically deny the existence of natural rights, he does insist that "abstract right" is not the proper ethical foundation for liberty. Put more simply, Bentham may be correct that there is no such thing as a "natural" right, but even if natural rights do exist, Mill's particular species of liberalism does not rely on them. Second, Mill avers that the authoritative foundation for liberty is to be found in "utility." The justification for why people should be given liberty (or not) stems from the assumption that its consequences are desirable, not any sense that it is intrinsically valuable. And finally, the particular version of utilitarianism upon which Mill rests his moral and political philosophy differs from Bentham's crude hedonism. Rather than a subjective calculus of the magnitude of pleasure and pain, the ultimate utility of ethical questions can only be measured against the "permanent interests" of mankind's ongoing moral and civilizational progress.

Even in the context of *On Liberty*, Mill's utilitarianism leads him to what appears to be, in light of the first three chapters of the book, several jarring policy prescriptions in Chapters 4 and 5. Among many potentially illiberal 'applications" of the theory of liberty, Mill condones something akin to mandatory drug testing for those in positions of public responsibility; workfare and compulsory child support; ongoing legal restrictions on people who commit violent crimes while under the influence of alcohol or drugs; the criminalization of public indecency; laws prohibiting solicitation or the operation of brothels and gambling houses; the denial of marriage licenses to the poor; mandatory education of children according to state standards; and so forth.[9]

In all of these instances, Mill's case for regulation hinges on the notion that with respect to actions that have potentially deleterious consequences for others, or in cases where we have violated a "distinct and assignable obligation," society has the right to hold us accountable in the name of the public good.[10] Nor are libertarian appeals to the absolute or inalienable character of liberty considered valid objections. Mill dismisses the "misplaced notions of liberty" that are invoked by way of shirking societal obligations, even to the point of insisting that "one of the cases in which, in the modern European world, the sentiment of liberty is the strongest [i.e., with respect to children and the family], is a case where, in my view, it is altogether misplaced."[11]

Among the vexing corollaries of Mill's utilitarian liberalism is the suggestion, in *On Liberty* and elsewhere, that humans are deserving of freedom not as an inalienable birthright or entitlement, but rather on the empirical assumption that without liberty, there is very little possibility for human progress. In this view, liberty looks to be nothing more than a necessary means—and an insufficient one at that—for the cultivation of individuality and progressive moral development, which is the primary goal of *On Liberty*. Even a society whose individuals enjoy a great latitude of formal liberty may not be able to overcome the "social tyranny" of custom, public opinion, or the vapid homogeneity of democratic culture.[12] Something more than just liberty—perhaps we might call it empowerment, character, or stimulation—is required to make sure that liberty gets translated into the goods Mill anticipates from it. Where these underlying conditions are otherwise lacking, the state may be required to supply them.

The broad system of *On Liberty*, then, is one in which liberty is extended—or withdrawn—depending on whether it is conducive to individual moral development. Conversely, in cases where liberty proves detrimental to the well-being of the subjects, or gets in the way of them satisfying their legitimate duties to society, there is no categorical reason in Mill's system why that liberty may not be abridged. As in the hypothetical case of a person who might forcibly be prevented from crossing an unsafe bridge, "liberty," Mill notes, "consists in doing what one desires, and he does not desire to fall into the river."[13] In this instance, Mill goes on to qualify, so long as the danger is not imminent, "the person himself can judge of the sufficiency . . . of the risk." But he leaves open the possibility that for those such as children, the insane, colonial subjects, or others allegedly incapable of the "full use of the reflecting faculty," one may legitimately make decisions on their behalf—and "without any *real* infringement of . . . liberty"![14]

Marginal cases of children, the mentally incompetent, the labor-
ing classes in England, or various colonial subjects who vegetate in
a kind of civilizational "non-age" that precludes them being "capable
of being improved by free and equal discussion" may seem to be
peripheral to Mill's general point about the principle of liberty.[15] Still,
they are indicative of discordant impulses in Mill's analysis, which
seem to lead in two very different directions with respect to liberty.
The first is that so long as an individual is of mature age and sound
faculties, she ought to be trusted to make her own decisions. Rightly
or wrongly, it is important that individuals be allowed to choose
for themselves. The second and more troubling notion, however, is
Mill's acknowledgment that an individual's desires may be faulty or
suspect, and that remonstrances, if not outright "despotism," may
sometimes be justifiable whenever the danger is sufficiently grave or
the individual's faculties are unreliable.[16]

The Efficiency of Economic Liberty:
The Utilitarian Case for Laissez-Faire

For Mill, the case of *economic* liberty represents a subset—albeit an
important one—of his broader discussion of freedom. It is important
to recall that the extent of liberty defended in *On Liberty* hinges on
a crucial distinction between a "sphere of action" that is by its very
nature "personal" or "self-regarding," that is, actions which pertain to
none other than the actor himself, and other conduct that is in Mill's
terms "social," meaning behavior that has consequences—whether
immediate or distant—for other people.[17] Whether conduct is
purely self-regarding or generates externalities that potentially affect
others is decisive for determining if and when society may intervene.

He is crystal clear that the virtually unlimited liberty extolled in
the first part of *On Liberty* pertains to conduct that is self-regarding.
Speech, expression, religious belief, and publication of specula-
tive ideas bear solely on the actor himself.[18] Only in extraordinary
cases, such as someone crying fire in a crowded theater or incendi-
ary speech in the midst of an angry mob, can speech have negative
externalities for others.[19] As Thomas Jefferson famously said, my

neighbor's view of religious salvation "neither picks my pocket nor breaks my leg."[20] And yet beyond the strict category of self-regarding actions, the vast majority of human conduct affects other people. Mill is no fool in deeming every man a Robinson Crusoe, and he concedes that almost every action has indirect consequences, some of which may be pernicious.[21] Even so, "The acts of an individual may be hurtful to others, or wanting in due consideration for their welfare, without going the length of violating any of their constituted rights," and in cases like these, Mill holds that society must be willing to bear the "merely contingent" harm for the sake of the "greater good of human freedom."[22]

The flip side of this doctrine, however, is that "as soon as any part of a person's conduct affects prejudicially the interests of others, society has jurisdiction over it, and the question of whether the general welfare will or will not be promoted by interfering with it, becomes open to discussion."[23] Mill allows that "in all things which regard the external relations of the individual, he is *de jure* amenable to those whose interests are concerned, and if need be, to society as their protector."[24] So from the vantage of social regulation, the issue is not whether in fact society has jurisdiction over prejudicial conduct, but rather the more complicated pragmatic matter of when the goods of acting on that power outweigh the drawbacks. This is not a question that lends itself to a categorical solution. Many cases fall "on the exact boundary line between two principles."[25] "Whenever," Mill admits, "there is a definite damage, or a definite risk of damage, either to an individual or the public, the case is taken out of the province of liberty, and placed in that of morality or law."[26]

Commerce is chief among the kinds of social conduct that Mill deems amenable to social regulation. He stipulates that "trade is a social act," and as such, it belongs in a different class than the self-regarding freedoms defended in *On Liberty*. "Whoever undertakes to sell any description of goods to the public, does what affects the interests of other persons, and society in general; and *thus his conduct, in principle, comes within the jurisdiction of society*."[27] Chapter 5 of *On Liberty* reveals that the vaunted cause of "'Free Trade' . . . rests on grounds different from, though equally solid with, the principle of individual liberty asserted in this Essay."[28] Mill further clarifies that "restrictions on trade . . . are indeed restraints; and all restraint, *qua restraint, is an evil.*" Nonetheless, and this is key, "*the restraints in question affect only that part of conduct which society is competent to restrain,* and are wrong *solely* because they do not really produce the results which it is desired to produce by them."[29] There is no principled reason why society may not regulate commerce in pursuit of public goods such as health, safety, or sanitation.[30] Whether it is *prudent* for it to do so, however, is another question that appeals to a register of considerations altogether different than those involved in the question of liberty. These are the sorts of criteria raised by Mill in his work on political economy.

Mill's *Principles of Political Economy: With Some of Their Applications to Social Philosophy* (1848) has traditionally been seen as supportive of private ownership, laissez-faire, and voluntary association. In the course of *Principles*, Mill advances a number of powerful arguments on behalf of economic liberty. First, when it comes to legislation or regulation, there are good reasons to assume that individuals and voluntary associations will do a better job of providing collective goods than governments.[31] Mill affirms the familiar classical liberal position that "the great majority of things are worse done by the intervention of government, than the individuals most interested in the matter would do them, or cause them to be done, if left to themselves."[32] Moreover, and here echoing Tocqueville, a society where all significant activities have been absorbed by government is one that is likely to be devoid of energy, creativity, or public spirit.[33] "*Laissez-faire,*" Mill declares, "should be the general practice: every departure from it, unless required by some great good, is a certain evil."[34]

These positions all bolster the case for Mill as an apostle of economic liberty. However, in another light one might argue that Mill takes a wrong turn by resting the case for economic liberty squarely on grounds of its putative efficiency. By hitching their wagons to hypothesized assumptions about the superior—if not perfect—efficiency of free markets, Mill and his legatees potentially conflate an empirical fact (or indeed a hypothetical construct) with a normative principle. What if it turns out that markets are manifestly inefficient? Or that human beings are fallible creatures who err even in their own personal affairs? If the *only* reason why governments may not abridge economic liberty is the allegedly superior efficiency of free markets, then the whole normative edifice undergirding economic freedom may be weakened by counterexamples of market inefficiencies or human irrationality. Subsequent discoveries in behavioral economics seem to confirm the irrationality of economic actors—not to mention the misallocations of capital that result from manias, bubbles, and panics. Palpable market failures and inefficiencies open the door to opponents of economic liberty, who contend that the state might very well do a better job preventing some of the most egregious examples of economic irrationality, or that people need to be "nudged" into behaving more intelligently.[35]

In sum, while Mill and contemporary defenders of spontaneous order and the miracles of the market may be broadly correct that the market does the best job of allocating goods and resources, efficiency can't possibly be the only grounds for supporting economic freedom. Not only is this view Panglossian, but it ignores the inherent dignity of human liberty and the importance of allowing individuals to manage their own affairs. *Even if* markets prove to be inefficient from time to time, and humans are revealed to be incorrigibly self-destructive, it is still important to allow them to pursue their dreams and to take responsibility for their own decisions. Economic liberty must be valued for its own sake.

Private Property as Natural or Social?

One of the centerpieces of classical liberalism in the 17th and 18th centuries was its commitment to the institution of private property. For Locke, famously, individuals hold a property in themselves, and natural law entitles them to the fruits of their labor. From a broader vantage, the Greek, Roman, and Christian traditions all maintained that the institution of private property was both natural and, consequently, desirable.[36] While Mill appears generally favorable to property rights, he also shows an alarming openness to the collectivist notion that systems of property are historical artifacts—susceptible to being reformed or redistributed in light of the cumulative knowledge of mankind. The *Autobiography* reveals the enduring impression the St. Simonians left on Mill with respect to the question of private property. As he recalls:

> Their criticisms on the common doctrines of Liberalism seemed to me full of important truth; it was partly by their writings that my eyes were opened to the very limited and temporary value of the old political economy, which assumes private property and inheritance as indefeasible facts, and freedom of production and exchange as the *dernier mot* of social improvement.[37]

Mill goes on to praise their aims as "desirable and rational," even as he confesses that he could fully endorse neither the practicality nor efficacy of the "social machinery" required to effect this transformation. Even so, he concludes that as impracticable as it seems at present, the St. Simonian "ideal of human society" might serve as an inspiration "to the efforts of others to bring society, as at present constituted, nearer to some ideal standard."[38]

This was no mere youthful enthusiasm, as successive editions of *Principles* bear the imprimatur of these socialistic ideas. Both the institution of private property and its present distribution are altogether fungible:

> The distribution of wealth . . . is a matter of human institution solely. The things once there, mankind, individually or collectively, can do with them as they like. They can place them at the disposal of whomsoever they please, and on whatever terms. . . . Even what a person has produced by his individual toil, unaided by any one, he cannot keep, unless by the permission of society. Not only can society take it from him, but individuals could and would take it from him, if society only remained passive. . . . The distribution of wealth, therefore, depends on the laws and customs of society. The rules by which it is determined, are what the opinions and feelings of the ruling portion of the community make them, and are very

different in different ages and countries; and might be still more different if mankind so chose.[39]

What, then, determines whether society ought to be content with prevailing systems of ownership? Or, put differently, why should we prefer private property to some other more collectivistic arrangement of the future? Mill's response is hardly reassuring. The sole criterion for arbitrating between different systems of property ownership seems to be whether a particular system is conducive to the perfection of "intelligence and the moral faculties." Whether "individual agency in its best form" or some variant of socialism will prove superior in satisfying these needs is a "mere question of comparative advantages, which futurity must determine."[40] For Mill, the question of "which of the two will be the ultimate form of human society" remains open.[41] Again we are thrown back—as in the question of liberty itself—on amorphous notions of "progress," "development," and "improvement" as the benchmarks of social policy.

Likewise, Mill seizes on an ambiguity in the classical liberal doctrine of the right of property being derived from labor. If labor is supposedly what generates the natural sanction for ownership, what do we do with the legal institution of inheritance—which grants property to those who did not labor for it? This is an even more acute issue with the inheritance of landed property, where neither the surplus value produced by the land itself, nor exclusive ownership by individuals who may or may not be laborers or improvers, is self-evidently deducible from the original labor theory. "The essential principle of property being to assure to all persons what they have produced by their labour and accumulated by their abstinence," it is hard to apply this doctrine to the "raw material of the earth."[42] Alluding to the Lockean account, Mill notes, "In no sound theory of private property was it ever contemplated that the proprietor of land should be merely a sinecurist quartered on it" rather than a legitimate improver.[43] Far from condoning doctrines of the "'sacredness of property,'" Mill grudgingly concludes that only the expediency of the institution of landed property is sufficient to outweigh its inherent injustice.[44]

In keeping with his broader animus against irrational and inherited political privileges, Mill similarly rejects the economic institution of inheritance. The ability to pass along one's property to a descendant or series of descendants in perpetuity smacks of "the feudal family, the last historical form of patriarchal life."[45] This feudal world must give way to that of modern individualism, and inheritance laws are legitimate tools for equalizing unearned advantages. As he remarks, "the inequalities of property which arise from unequal industry, frugality, perseverance, talents, and to a certain extent even opportunities, are inseparable from the principle of private property, and if we accept the principle, we must bear with these consequences of it." However, "I see nothing objectionable in fixing a limit to what any one may acquire by the mere favour of others, without any exercise of his faculties, and in requiring that if he desires any further accession of fortune, he shall work for it."[46]

De Gustibus Non Est Disputandum?
On Higher and Lower Tastes

On Liberty counsels that we should be cautious about gainsaying the preferences of others. Knowledge is fallible, a hodgepodge of mere opinions, half-truths, and non-truths that can at best approximate "Truth" over the long haul. Ideas that seem outlandish or absurd in one age become the reigning orthodoxy of another, and vice versa. Even in rare circumstances when people express views that are demonstrably false or morally monstrous, we are obliged to stand aside and respect the rights of heretics and iconoclasts. Like the devil's advocate, they do us a great service.[47] What is important is not so much that one's opinion be correct as that it be one's own.[48] Authenticity, as much as falsifiability, emerges as the standard for Millian knowledge.

This strong view of the indeterminacy of human knowledge looks congenial to the epistemological premises of neoclassical or Austrian economics—what is known as the "subjective theory of value" captured by the Latin phrase "de gustibus non est disputandum."[49] From the vantage of much of contemporary economy theory, there's no disputing preferences. Subjective preferences are to be respected as "given" based on the assumptions that the actor is likely to have superior information than disinterested outsiders, and any attempt to substitute or improve on the preferences of individuals does violence to the value of human judgment. More fundamentally, because of the impossibility of making interpersonal value comparisons, preferences are incommensurable. There is no single scalar according to which one preference may be said to be better or worse, more or less valid, than any other.

We might expect Mill to share this agnosticism with respect to the value of individual preferences. And yet his considered view seems to be just the opposite. Individuals should not be deprived of their preferences by force or regulation, but this is not to say that one cannot distinguish between higher and lower tastes. Indeed the broader notion of civilizational progress to which Mill is committed aims to elevate the preferences of ordinary individuals. Denying the crude hedonism often associated with utilitarianism, Mill insists that "it is quite compatible with the principle of utility to recognize the fact, that some *kinds* of pleasures are more desirable and valuable than others."[50] Wherein consists the "intrinsic superiority" of the higher to the lower goods? Their superiority is demonstrated by the consensus of "all or almost all who have experience of both" and who are "equally capable of appreciating and enjoying" a particular good. Such a "being of higher faculties" has managed to cultivate the "capacity for nobler feelings."[51]

Mill's break with Bentham's hedonism is immortalized by his incredulity toward his mentor's notion that "quantity of pleasure being equal, push pin is as good as poetry."[52] Far better, Mill contends, to be Socrates unsatisfied than a sated sow.[53] As we've seen above, within the limits of the harm principle, Mill is committed to protecting the rights of individuals to pursue lower tastes and desires. At the same time, however, Mill ushers in a way of looking at the world by which certain authorities—legislators, intellectuals, philosophers, educators, etc.—ought to be committed to improving the tastes and preferences of the rude and uncultivated masses. The upshot for Mill: elites and experts often do know better than regular folks.

There are echoes of this elitist sensibility in Mill's vision of the market and his support for certain kinds of regulations. Ordinarily people's tastes and desires in the marketplace should be respected. And yet only in certain rudimentary areas is the consumer a competent judge of goods or commodities produced for his desires and needs.[54] Because of this discrepancy between the expressed preferences of uncultivated individuals and their true needs, the government may have to act to ensure the provision of some goods. Mill invokes the existence of certain "things of the worth of which the demand of the market is by no means a test."[55] These are sublime goods "whose utility does not consist in ministering to inclinations, nor in serving the daily uses of life, and the want of which is least felt where the need is greatest."[56] All that is to say that certain goods—indeed perhaps even the most important goods—must be provided for the people even though there is no immediate demand for them.

These goods include matters of personal cultivation such as education. They also include non-immediate goods such as retirement or saving for the future that are so far off on the horizon that one cannot reasonably expect people to place any weight on them given the natural tendency to discount the future.[57] They also include many instances that require overcoming a collective action problem such as agitating for higher pay or fewer hours for labor.[58] In all these instances, Mill allows that there is some role for government intervention, whether to provide for goods that people should value at present but, for some reason, do not, or alternatively, to disabuse them of their preference for something that they do want but ought not to value so highly.

Commerce and Character: The Millian Ambivalence Toward Commerce

Material improvement is one of the great benchmarks of civilization. We know a civilized society, at least in part, by the fact that it has achieved a certain degree of wealth. As Mill notes in the essay "Civilization," the growth of industry, infrastructure, and economic well-being are necessary conditions for the progressive development of civilization.[59] Civilization requires cooperation, and it is this ability to combine one's self with others and to work collectively that allows civilized nations to undertake great projects and improve the world.[60] Civilization also demands that one be willing and able to subordinate short-term desires and passions to longer-term interests.[61] As do 18th-century thinkers such as David Hume and Adam Smith, Mill accepts that commerce plays a role in fostering characterological habits of moderation, self-control, sobriety, prudence, and judgment that make civilization possible.

Mill credits what he calls the "business of life" for focusing the attention and training the minds of ordinary citizens. In reckoning with their personal affairs, pursuing desirable enterprises, making their own decisions, and confronting the "difficulties of life," ordinary citizens acquire skills and competencies that help them to develop and mature as human beings. Commerce stimulates the "vigorous exercise of the active energies; labour, contrivance, judgment, self-control." Unless we are allowed to take responsibility for everyday decisions, our faculties remain "only half-developed," morally and politically stunted in some respect.[62]

One of the great puzzles of Mill's philosophy is why he does not draw a stronger link between the spirit of invention, ingenuity, and iconoclasm he extols in the realm of ideas and the competitive market economy. He avidly celebrates the accomplishments of eccentric individuals who "think different" when it is a matter of challenging religious orthodoxy or espousing controversial ideas. The discoveries of these rare and beautiful geniuses all redound to the improvement of mankind. Yet not only does Mill fail to make the connection between the iconoclastic energy he celebrates in the realm of ideas and the creative destruction of the marketplace. He seems to regard authentic individuality and modern commercial society as mutually antithetical. Like his fellow "aristocratic liberal" Tocqueville, Mill regards modern commercial society with a degree of condescension, if not outright disdain.[63]

Despite the occasional nod toward the ennobling functions of commerce and everyday affairs, Mill portrays modern commercial society as ushering in a degree of homogeneity and uniformity that is more stifling than invigorating. Among the "great mass of influences hostile to individuality" Mill cites the "increase of commerce and manufactures," which democratizes the spirit of ambition and opens the pursuit of social advancement to everyone in society.[64] This leads to the extinction of "energetic characters on any large scale," a consequence of the fact that "there is now scarcely any outlet for energy in this country except business." While conceding that the amount of energy devoted to business may be "considerable," what little exertion remains leftover is squandered on hobbies, philanthropy, or some other "thing of small dimension."[65]

Competition in the realm of ideas yields progress, but not so in the business world. There competition leads to "quackery" and "puffing"—Mill's demeaning terms for salesmanship. Modern society is characterized by an "intensity of competition," which "drives the public more and more to play high for success," resulting in greater fraud, hucksterism, bankruptcy, and other heretofore "disgraceful" behaviors that begin to lose whatever salutary stigma they may have had in an earlier age.[66] The honest local tradesmen of a bygone era are gradually driven out of business by sharp-elbowed new entrepreneurs hawking generic, low-quality products through a mix of aggressive underselling, corner-cutting, and shameless self-promotion. According to Mill, these and other pathologies are the "inevitable fruits of immense competition."[67]

Whereas the stifling homogeneity and middling ambitions of a commercial society are bad, Mill does allow that Tocquevillean "soft despotism" is far worse. "Even if," Mill hypothesizes, "the government could comprehend within itself . . . all the most eminent intellectual capacity and active talent of the nation, it would not be the less desirable that the conduct of a large portion of the affairs of society should be left in the hands of the persons immediately interested in them."[68] Supposing hypercompetent bureaucrats could do a better job than private individuals, Mill urges that "it is nevertheless desirable that it should be done by them, rather than the government, as a means to their own mental education—a mode of strengthening their active faculties, exercising their judgment, and giving them a familiar knowledge of the subjects with which they are thus left to deal."[69]

Like Tocqueville, Mill worries that if the administrative state absorbs every function, society will be sapped of energy, and a torpid uniformity will befall society. In contrast to the actions of "individuals and voluntary associations," which are characterized by "varied experiments and endless diversity of experience," the workings of government "tend to be everywhere alike."[70] Again following Tocqueville, Mill sensibly recommends the spirit of voluntary association as a tool for combating the drift toward administrative centralization. Association is the watchword of the future, and centralization is to be resisted as anathema.[71] Even here, though, Mill worries that the Tocquevillean prescription of groups and association may be a cure worse than the disease, as groups—especially political parties—tend to produce unreflective conformity and "ape-like . . . imitation."[72] Rather than encouraging groups, cultivating "beautiful" individuals is the answer.[73]

For all of his talk about radical individuality and the disproportionate importance of eccentric geniuses, though, Mill is curiously unaware of the potential affinity between his Humboldtian affirmation of individual spontaneity, novelty, and development, on the one hand, and the creative aspects of entrepreneurship and economic competition, on the other. We hear much praise for the achievements of Socrates, Luther, and Copernicus, but there is precious little in Mill celebrating the likes of a Sam Walton, Warren Buffett, Steve Jobs, or Bill Gates.

Conclusion: The Paradox of Millian Liberalism

Notwithstanding his undeniable brilliance and his eloquent defense of individual liberty, Mill occupies an uneasy place within the liberal tradition. Like contemporary liberals, Mill is a steadfast defender of certain kinds of preferred freedoms such as speech, expression, and religious belief. He also appreciates the neoclassical and Austrian case for why markets are likely, on the whole, to do a better job allocating goods and resources than arbitrary legislation or well-meaning technocrats. At the same time, however, the philosophical under-pinnings of Mill's arguments—ranging from his developmental version of utilitarianism, his emphasis on elevating human preferences rather than taking them as given, and his aristocratic suspicion of the tension between commerce and character—make him an ambivalent liberal, if not quite the outright harbinger of collectivism identified by Hayek and Mises.

Notes

1. Elie Halévy, *The Growth of Philosophical Radicalism* (London: Faber and Faber, 1949); and F. A. Hayek, *The Constitution of Liberty* (Chicago: 1960), 8, 30, 174, and 394. For a more nuanced treatment of Hayek's complex and evolving assessments of Mill, see especially Bruce Caldwell, "Hayek on Mill," *History of Political Economy* 40 (2008): 689–704.

2. See especially Hayek, *The Fatal Conceit: The Errors of Socialism* (Chicago: University of Chicago Press, 1988), esp. 52, 65, 92–93, and 148–49, where he repeatedly refers to Mill as the "saint of rationalism."

3. For example, L. T. Hobhouse, *Liberalism* (Oxford: Oxford University Press, 1911), chaps. 5 and 6; and Harold J. Laski, *The Rise of European Liberalism* (London: Allen & Unwin, 1936), 241.

4. Joseph Hamburger, *John Stuart Mill on Liberty and Control* (Princeton: Princeton University Press, 2000).

5. Hayek's assessment mirrors Laski's above: both concur that Mill "probably led more intellectuals into socialism than any other single person," including Marx. See Hayek, *The Fatal Conceit*, 149.

6. J. S. Mill, *Autobiography* (Boston: Houghton Mifflin, 1969), 60–61.

7. Jeremy Bentham, "Anarchical Fallacies," in *The Collected Works of Jeremy Bentham*, vol. 2, ed. John Bowring (Edinburgh: William Tait, 1843), 502.

8. John Stuart Mill, *On Liberty*, in *On Liberty and Other Essays*, ed. John Gray (Oxford: Oxford World Classics, 1991), 15.

9. Ibid., 90–91, 106–12, and 115–21.

10. Ibid., 90.

11. Ibid., 116.

12. Ibid., 8–9, 65–68, 70–73, and 80–81.

13. Ibid., 106–7.

14. Ibid., 95.

15. Ibid., 14–15 and 114–20. See also Mill, *Principles of Political Economy, with Some of Their Applications to Social Philosophy* (1848; New York: Appleton, 1923), vol. 2, Book V, chap. 11, pp. 577–81.

16. Mill, *On Liberty*, 14–15.

17. Ibid., 16, 83–84, and 86–89.

18. Ibid., 16–17.

19. For Mill's analogue of this exception, see ibid., 62: "No one pretends that actions should be as free as opinions. On the contrary, even opinions lose their immunity, when the circumstances in which they are expressed are such as to constitute their expression a positive instigation to some mischievous act."

20. Thomas Jefferson, in *Notes on the State of Virginia*, ed. William Peden (Chapel Hill, NC: University of North Carolina Press, 1955), 159.

21. Mill, *On Liberty*, 88–89.

22. Ibid., 83 and 91.

23. Ibid., 84.

24. Ibid., 16.

25. Ibid., 110.

26. Ibid., 91.

27. Ibid., 105 (emphasis added).

28. Ibid.

29. Ibid. (emphasis added).

30. Ibid., 106.

31. Mill, *Principles of Political Economy*, vol. 2, Book V, chap. 11, pp. 565–67.

32. Ibid., 565.

33. Ibid., 567–69.

34. Ibid., 569.

35. See, for example, Richard Thaler and Cass Sunstein, *Nudge: Improving Decisions About Health, Wealth, and Happiness* (New York: Penguin, 2009).

36. Richard Schlatter, *Private Property: The History of an Idea* (New Brunswick, NJ: Rutgers University Press, 1951); and Alan Ryan, *Property and Political Theory* (Oxford: Blackwell, 1984).

37. Mill, *Autobiography*, 100.

38. Ibid., 100–1.

39. Mill, *Principles of Political Economy*, vol. 1, Book II, chap. 1, p. 258.

40. Ibid., 269.

41. Ibid., 269–71.

42. Ibid., chap. 2, p. 291.

43. Ibid., 293.

44. Ibid., 294–95.

45. Ibid., 282.

46. Ibid., 289.

47. Mill, *On Liberty*, 21–27, 43, and 48–54.

48. Ibid., 40–41 and 64–65.

49. On the subjective theory of value, see especially Carl Menger, *Principles of Economics* (1871; Auburn, AL: Mises Institute, 2007).

50. John Stuart Mill, "Utilitarianism," in *On Liberty and Other Essays.*

51. Ibid.," 139 and 141.

52. John Stuart Mill, "Bentham," in *Dissertations and Discussions: Political, Philosophical, and Historical*, vol. 1 (London: Parker, 1859), 389.

53. Mill, "Utilitarianism," 140.

54. Mill, *Principles of Political Economy*, vol. 2, Book V, chap. 11, p. 573.

55. Ibid.

56. Ibid., 573–74.

57. Ibid., 581.

58. Ibid., 585–87.

59. John Stuart Mill, "Civilization," in *The Collected Works of John Stuart Mill*, vol. 18, ed. John Robson (Toronto: University of Toronto Press, 1977), 119–22.

60. Ibid., 120 and 122.

61. Ibid., 122–31.

62. Mill, *Principles of Political Economy*, 567.

63. On the affinities between these thinkers with respect to their "aristocratic" sensibilities and aversion to mass society, see especially Alan Kahan, *Aristocratic Liberalism: The Social and Political Thought of Jacob Burckhardt, John Stuart Mill, and Alexis de Tocqueville* (New York: Oxford University Press, 1992).

64. Mill, *On Liberty*, 81.

65. Ibid., 77–78.

66. Mill, "Civilization," 133.

67. Ibid., 133.

68. Mill, *Principles of Political Economy*, vol. 2, Book V, chap. 11, pp. 566–67.

69. Mill, *On Liberty*, 121.

70. Ibid., 122.

71. See, for example, John Stuart Mill, "Centralisation," in *The Collected Works of John Stuart Mill*, vol. 19, pp. 579–615.

72. Mill, *On Liberty*, 22–23, 65, and 73–75.

73. Mill, *On Liberty*, 70 and 74.

Economic Liberty as Anti-Flourishing: Marx and Especially His Followers

DEIRDRE NANSEN MCCLOSKEY

University of Illinois at Chicago (professor emerita)

Karl Marx has had since 1848 the tightest grip on the social imaginary of the clerisy out of all the men we are discussing here.[1] He famously declared that he was not a Marxist. But his followers are Marxists still, in departments of history and English, in cultural studies and economic development. The followers, many of them among my dearest friends, are not always declared Marxists, or even, to assign a name to a less rigorous position, "Marxian"—people cheerfully influenced by Marx, though not so cheerful about Stalin or Mao. And beyond the various ranks of official believers, the implicit followers during the age of materialism, 1890 to 1980—"Marxoids" one might say, without intending to sneer—included most social thinkers, not all of them on the left.

In the early and mid-20th century in progressive and a good deal of conservative writing of history, for example, the prevailing rhetoric wished *always* to see motives of class and economics hidden behind *every* professed sentiment. You can see it in Charles Beard's *An Economic Interpretation of the Constitution* (1913) or Georges Lefebvre's *Quatre-vingt-neuf* (Seventeen eighty-nine), translated as *The Coming of the French Revolution* (1939), or Christopher Hill's *The English Revolution 1640* (1940).[2] It was a reaction to the nationalist tradition in Romantic writing of history. "Aha, you alleged 'patriot,' you 'liberal,'" declared the hard-nosed anti-Romantics under the spell of Marx the inverted Romantic, "You can't fool us. We see your economic interest behind your so-called ideas." Even anti-Marxians such as the British historian Hugh Trevor-Roper, ennobled by Margaret Thatcher and famous for his opposition to materialist explanations of the English Civil War (what Hill had called a revolution), wished in his first book, in 1940 on Charles I's Archbishop Laud, to slip in at the outset a quantitative estimate of 100 percent for profane prudence as against the faith or courage celebrated by Jules Michelet or Thomas Carlyle or John Lothrop Motley or Thomas Babbington Macaulay. Trevor-Roper conceded on page 3 that "political ambition is only one among" the instincts sublimated in religion under Charles I. Yet he continued, "in politics it is naturally by far the most potent."[3] Well, sometimes. You don't know on page 3.

The American appeals court judge Learned Hand said in 1944, "The spirit of liberty is the spirit which is not too sure that it is right; the spirit of liberty is the spirit which seeks to understand the minds of other men and women."[4] In 1983, the philosopher Amélie Oksenberg Rorty reaffirmed it as a crucial principle for coming to know truly, namely:

> our ability to engage in continuous conversation, testing one another, discovering our hidden presuppositions, changing our minds because we have listened to the voices of our fellows. Lunatics also change their minds, but their minds change with the tides of the moon and not because they have listened, really listened, to their friends' questions and objections.[5]

Admitting that there's enough blame for voluntary deafness to go quite around the political spectrum, the followers of Marx have since 1848 seldom adhered to such principles, and less so now it seems than once—although I am lovingly acquainted with splendid exceptions (listen up George, Jack, Steve, and David).[6] Some years ago I mildly remarked to a gathering of my beloved Department of English at the University of Illinois at Chicago that the speaker who had just concluded his presentation, a fashionable Marxian imported from New York, just might not have got the economic history exactly right. The speaker responded in a sentence, "Oh, I see that you are a neoliberal" and sat down. That was it, and none of my colleagues, mostly themselves Marxians or Marxoids or cautious fellow travelers, would speak up to insist that he respond more fully to someone who after all had some claim to knowing a little about economics and history. I was startled by his exhibition of proud ignorance and saddened by the implicit agreement in the room that one is *not* to "listen, really listen, to one's friends' questions and objections" and certainly not to those of one's party enemies. The result of a century of name-calling-as-argument, from "Bernsteinian revisionism" and "economism" to "bourgeois" and "neoliberal," and not listening, really listening, has had the scientific result one might expect. In a cartoon cover of the *National Review* by Thomas Reis in August 2014, a supercool little Karl Marx, with a Starbucks coffee in his hand and an MP3 player in his ear and a jaunty hat on his head, sports a T-shirt inscribed, "Still Wrong."[7] Right.

Yet I enrage my friends on the right by stating the obvious, that Marx was the greatest social scientist of the 19th century, without compare. But then I enrage my friends on the left by adding, which is my point here, that he was nonetheless mistaken on almost every point of economics and of history. Which is why I haven't got any friends.

That second enraging fact is what we need to understand, for its present use. In their persistence in scientific error the followers of Marx are more interesting than the man himself, who after all tried hard to use his amazing intellect to see to the bottom of what was then known of economics and of history. It was to be expected, considering the state then of economics and of history, that he would get many points wrong. For example, his foundational labor theory of value was wrong, as every serious student of the matter has agreed for the past century and a half. The Blessed Smith himself had introduced the notion, and it was still believed by such splendid figures as David Ricardo and John Stuart Mill, Mill being a contemporary of Marx. But neither Mill nor Marx had the benefit of the Neoclassical Revolution in the history of economic thought during the 1870s. It developed in the works of Walras, Jevons, and Menger the correct view, confirmed thereafter in a thousand scientific studies, that value is determined by how much people want things, considering the income available, not by how much effort the seller put into the things, and that the wage is determined not by bargaining strength but by the market value of what the last worker produces, considering that free labor is a little mobile.

Why, then, is Marxism, or at any rate the materialist interpretation of history and an economics innocent of any analysis beyond *Das Kapital* in 1867, so persistent? Why haven't the Marxists, Marxians, and Marxoids, with a surprisingly small list of honorable exceptions—which does not include such eminent figures nowadays as David Harvey, Immanuel Wallerstein, and Frederic Jameson[8]—listened to their friends' questions and objections?

For one thing, the elements of Marxism are fairly easy to master, but sufficiently mysterious to attract young people, especially young men. St. Augustine, who had been a professor of rhetoric, wrote of the difficulties in the Bible that "I do not doubt that this situation was provided by God . . . to conquer disdain in our minds, to which those things which are easily discovered seem frequently to be worthless."[9] *Das Kapital*, especially the posthumous volumes II (1885) and III (1894),[10] is only read seriously by the devout.

For another, an identity as a leftist is acquired early and seems then hard to shed—although of course it is a truth of 20th-century biography that very many thoughtful people have gone from left to right, from socialism or regulation to conservatism or libertarianism, and vanishingly few the other way. Leszek Kołakowski, for example, was once in Poland an ardent young communist, as Robert Nozick was once a socialist.[11] I myself am a case in point of the usual direction. Having discovered at age 14 Prince Kropotkin's *Mutual Aid*[12] in the Carnegie-financed library in Wakefield, Massachusetts, I progressed rapidly through left anarchism and Trotskyism and left Democrat and social engineering, and then more slowly by the decades through conventional Chicago School economics to Austrian economics and at last to sisterly libertarianism and a new humanomics (so new and up-to-date as Adam Smith's *Theory of Moral Sentiments*, 1759).

The mechanism seems to be that, when a sensitive adolescent in a nonslave society first notices that some people are much poorer than her family, she is likely to conclude that the best remedy is to open

Daddy's wallet. (It is not an efficacious plan, because redistribution can give to the poor the mere 20 percent or so of the national income now in the hands of the wretchedly rich, and *one time only*, whereas trade-tested betterment under private property has given the poor, 1800 to the present, underestimated in the available measures, fully 3,000 percent, collected every year in now well-to-do countries filled with descendants of poor people.[13])

The historian Eric Hobsbawm (1917–2012), for instance, describes in his engaging autobiography of 2002 how he wanted to become a communist at age 14 and became one at 16—though, come to think of it, who would *not* in Germany in 1931 become something like a Communist?[14] Not anyone with a heart. (By 2002, true, one might inquire about the brain.) Hobsbawm pauses in his book from time to time to explain why, in the face of Stalin's crimes and the Hungarian uprising and the rest, he only ceased being a dues-paying if unorthodox member of the Communist Party of Great Britain a few months before it dissolved itself in 1991. His explanation, a strange one in such an intelligent man, is that he didn't want to give satisfaction to McCarthyites (whose British version had, to be sure, blocked him from many well-deserved academic appointments). He was faithful to the end—as people often are once their identities are formed, becoming uninterested in contrary facts that might be acquired after age 14. It is rather like the atheism at age 14 that bright boys and some bright girls espouse, never to be reconsidered, which then spills out of the mouths of 50-year-old men who have meanwhile not cracked a serious book on theology. Likewise, most of the Marxists and many of the Marxians and Marxoids have not cracked a serious book on economics published after 1867 or 1885 or 1894.

Marxism is like atheism, too (of course, it *is* atheism, as one may study in the reaction of the Chinese Communist Party to the Falun Gong), in appealing to a macho positivism, a minority view until the 1890s even among the clerisy, but coming into wide favor in the ethics-denying generation stunned by the Great War. As Bernard Williams said about the temptations facing the amoralist, 'he must resist, if consistent [in claiming that ethics is bosh], . . . [a] tendency to think of himself as being in character really rather splendid—in particular, as being by comparison with the craven multitude notably courageous," standing alone against the soft and bourgeois conventions of ethics.[15] Or as the conservative political philosopher J. Budziszinski puts it, describing his youthful and nihilistic self: "like Nietzsche, I imagined myself one of the few who could believe such things—who could walk the rocky heights where the air is thin and cold."[16] Courageously tough. On a British television show in 1994 Hobsbawm was asked by the liberal Michael Ignatieff whether "the murder of 15, 20 million people [in the USSR under Stalin] might have been justified" in light of its contribution to founding a communist society.[17] Hobsbawm *without hesitation* replied, "Yes." Hard-minded. Or party-line-ish. Or thuggish. Oh, Eric.

⸙

A Marxian will object to all this that she espouses historical materialism not because of her identity formed at age 14 as a leftist ("a good social democrat," she will say in a revealing phrase, the conservatives or libertarians being of course bad and anti-poor) but because Marx was substantially, scientifically correct, giving a correct analysis of the past and present and future.

Yet she is mistaken, scientifically. The American humorist Josh Billings long ago said, "It's better to know less than to know so much that ain't so." Daron Acemoglu's and James Robinson's *Why Nations Fail* (2012), to take a recent example of the persistence of a Marxoid just-so story, has much in it with which to agree: Europe's advance was highly contingent; political and economic liberty are linked; economic growth can't get going in the midst of a civil war. But Acemoglu and Robinson expressly and even a little proudly rely on a startlingly out-of-date account of the Industrial Revolution. "Our argument about the causes," they assert, "is highly influenced by" a list of "scholars in turn . . . inspired by earlier Marxist interpretations" of the 1920s through the 1960s, such as R. H. Tawney, Maurice Dobb, and Christopher Hill.[18] The *locus classicus* of such interpretations, and the introduction of the very phrase "the industrial revolution" into English, had been *Lectures on the Industrial Revolution of the Eighteenth Century in England* (1884), delivered by a university lecturer and ardent social reformer, Arnold Toynbee (1852–83), in 1882, the year before his death at age 31. Toynbee in turn depended on the story of triumph and tragedy put forward in *The Communist Manifesto*

For example, Toynbee (and then Tawney and Hobsbawm and Acemoglu and Robinson) declared that, "as a matter of fact, in the early days of competition,"

> the capitalists used all their power to oppress the laborers, and drove down wages to starvation point. This kind of competition has to be checked. . . . In England both remedies are in operation, the former through Trades Unions, the latter through factory legislation.[19]

None of this is true, though all of it fills the popular view of industrialization. There were no "early days of competition"—competition was common in any society of trade, as its enemies such as the medieval guildsmen sharply realized. Competition comes from entry, which is ancient, though of course irritating to those already rich from making new stone tools or new electronic computers. Competition, which sets one capitalist against another for our benefit, such as Uber and Lyft competing against taxi monopolies, needs to be encouraged, not checked.[20] Supply and demand, not 'power," is what determines wages, as one can see in the ups and downs of real wages in response to population downs and ups in the age of Malthus before 1798. The workers in the Industrial Revolution did not find their wages reduced and did not starve. England's last starvation time had been in the 1590s. Workers in the Industrial Revolution had moved eagerly to cities, not pushed by enclosures, even though Manchester and Lille and Boston were still even in Toynbee's time deathtraps of waterborne disease. Real wages in 1882 were in fact sharply rising and had not fallen in its run-up, before the legalization of trade unions. Children were being taken out of English factories well before the factory legislation began seriously to bite. Capital accumulation was not the heart of the Great Enrichment.

The just-so story is mistaken, as economic historians have established in the past century. In other words, Acemoglu and Robinson are accepting a mistaken leftish tale in economic history proposed in 1848 or 1867 or 1882 by brilliant amateurs before the professionalization of history, a story then rehearsed by Fabians at the hopeful height of the socialist idea, and then elaborated by a generation of (admittedly first-rate) Marxian historians, before thoroughgoing socialism had been tried and had failed, and before much of the scientific work had been done about the actual history—before it was realized, for instance, that other industrial revolutions occurred in, say, Islamic Spain or Sung China, as the historical sociologist Jack Goldstone observed in 2002: "Examined closely, many premodern and non-Western economies show spurts or efflorescences of economic growth, including sustained increases in both population and living standards, in urbanization, and in underlying technological change."[21]

꧁꧂

An instructive example of the pervasiveness of Marxian errors down to the present is *The Origins of Capitalism and the "Rise of the West*," a fine book of 2008 by sociological historian Eric Mielants. The historical and economic tale that Mielants tells is: The *relations of production* enable *capitalists* to extract *surplus value* from the *working class*. The *unequal bargaining power* of workers drives down wages.[22] Such an *exploitation of wage labor*[23] leads to profits, enlarged by *imperialist exploitation*.[24] Trade was *unequal exchange*[25] and resulted in an *unfavorable balance of trade*[26] between the *core* and the colonized *periphery*.[27] The profits thus acquired "achieve a *ceaseless accumulation of capital*,"[28] which is peculiar to *capitalism*.

All the italicized words are unrelated to how the world has actually worked. Everyone buying labor, for example, is a "capitalist" by a consistent use of the word, and therefore "exploiting." In the hungry 1930s the other Marx, the comedian Groucho, who had a cruel wit, denied a communist friend a job because, said Groucho with a smile, "Harry, I wouldn't want to exploit you." And so the peasant buying his neighbor's work at harvest time, which in the actual world has been noted since the first records we can read, in Mesopotamia around 2000 BCE, was a capitalist. Mielants conceives ancient trade as "providing some with profits while others were exploited."[29] But ask the inhabitants of the Indus valley civilization or those who traded with them in the third millennium BCE from the Horn of Africa or indirectly from Sumer if the trade was "exploitative." "Equal trade," a phrase that floats in the background of many Marxian discussions of exchange, sounds generously wise. It is not. We trade precisely because we differ—if you wish because of a species of "inequality"—not because we pointlessly trade your frog for my identical frog of equal value to us both.

In truth, after all, "surplus value" is "extracted" every time you exchange anything for something else—or else you wouldn't do it, would you, now? You are a "capitalist" when you buy a cup of coffee served by an "exploited" owner of a coffee shop. She gets the profit of a price higher than the lowest she would accept, and you get a cup of coffee for lower than the highest price you would accept—which is why exchange happens, earning a profit for both sides.

A member of the "working class," such as you or I, gets profit likewise from our employments. The working class in any case is not peculiar to modern times. It has existed anciently, as Mielants, who is in many ways an excellent scholar, admits for example in his careful review of actual archival scholarship on the medieval European economy. Under the Marxist definition of workers a CEO hired at $20,000,000 a year to drive Home Depot into the ditch is a worker, too, because he was hired. The "relations of production" therefore do not have the explanatory force that Marxists attribute to them. So the Marxist word "capitalist" and its derivative dating from Sombart, "capitalism," which are supposed to have historically unique relations of production, but don't, serve to mislead people into thinking that there is something especially modern about banking and finance and profits (which is mistaken, as Mielants, a fair-minded scholar I repeat, also points out; fourth-century Athens had banks[30]).

"Unequal bargaining power" and "unequal trade" can only mean market outcomes that we wish were different, wishing that the hungry farmer's cotton sold for 15 cents rather than 10 cents a pound, that the Indian worker got $10 an hour instead of pennies. No one bargains when they have options, and markets, as against literal enslavements, bring options, however nasty. An exit to another deal, in Albert Hirschman's terms,[31] is more efficacious outside of close relations than exercising voice, trying to bargain with the cashier at the local grocery store about the price of milk. The gain to be achieved from bargaining even between husband and wife is sharply limited if divorce is possible. If you don't like it, exit. Yes, I know: not costlessly. But that, too, is an economic point and open to quantitative estimation.

Outside of literal and therefore exitless slavery, or outside of very high transactions costs in getting to a competitor, or outside of legally enforced relationships (a closed union shop, for example, or a marriage without the right of divorce), people have choices, even if lamentably low incomes result because the economy in which they live has not adopted liberalism (in the old and European sense of free markets) for long enough to get to a Japanese or Botswanan standard of living. A poor child may have the choice of working as a messenger or as a rock-breaker, but in that case his rock-breaking employer can pay him no less than the going wage for messengers. The child will leave, exercising an (admittedly pathetic) right of exit. The Indian wage is lower than the American because the Indian economy is radically less productive, and because a worker sleeping on the streets of Mumbai cannot show up this afternoon for employment at a McDonald's in Chicago, not because the Indian worker has less bargaining power, or because American workers have more.

Choices by workers or their employers or the customers of their employers radically narrow the range of pure bargaining. Dockworkers in the western Swedish port of Gothenburg may indeed bargain for higher pay from the dock owners. In a closed shop the result comes exactly from their bargaining power, such as the power enforced by the state's monopoly of violence to prevent scabs from taking up the jobs of the dockers. But in the long run the temporarily better off Gothenburg dockers will drive their jobs to Copenhagen or Hamburg. So much for power as the main determinant of wages, a point that economists have been making at least since John R. Hicks' *The Theory of Wages*[32] in 1932, and in less explicit form since the Neoclassical Revolution. It applies in all markets with entry allowed. I may *want* to sell my house for $200,000, perhaps because that is what I paid for it at the peak of the housing boom. But if the other houses similar to it in the neighborhood—"comparables" in the jargon of realtors—now sell for $100,000, and if the buyers are moderately sensible and moderately free to exit, that's just too bad for me. The price of $100,000, plus or minus the merely few thousands achieved by skill in bargaining, is going to be the going price.

I didn't say I like the market outcomes every time, or that they bring on nirvana. I merely claim that trade-tested betterment has achieved since 1800 what the political scientist John Mueller calls a "pretty good" outcome of increasing income per head worldwide by 900 or 3,000 or 10,000 percent, depending on what part of the world you are talking about and how exactly you go about measuring the dimensions of the Great Enrichment.[33] Life expectancy has doubled. Literacy percentages have increased by a factor of eight. Pretty good. I do wish my house now sold for $200,000 and that Indian messengers now earned $10 an hour. (In a couple of generations, actually, if we and the Indians stick with roughly free markets, I reckon that both will come to pass.) I merely say, as Mielants himself puts it, that almost 'every market [is] governed by the laws of supply and demand."[34]

Even Mielants concedes that letting markets work has enriched poor people worldwide. Forty years ago, before the word "globalization" became common and before the word "neoliberalism" was known and before the wretched Washington Consensus and before the terrible Milton Friedman got his Nobel Prize in economics, the world faced a bottom 4 billion out of a total human population of merely 5 billion, with no prospects.[35] Now the abysmally poor are a bottom billion out of 7 billion, which is bad, but much, much better than in 1976, and historically unique. Since 1976, that is, most of the poorest people in the world have been getting better off almost every year. From 1981 to 2008 the share of the world's population living at the level of Afghanistan, a horrible $2 a day (expressed, if roughly, in present-day US prices allowing for the cost of living; US income now is $130 a day), fell from 70 percent to 42 percent.[36] The share of the world's population living on an appalling $1.25 a day, as in Liberia (the experiment in sending African Americans with longer American lineages than most European-origin Americans "back to Africa"), fell from 53 percent to 22 percent. It fell, in other words, by more than half. From 2005 to 2008 even sub-Saharan Africa, for the first time since its independence from the colonial powers half a century earlier, shared on average in the betterment.

It would be wonderful if the real wage did depend on the distribution of bargaining power—once unfair but now so easily corrected by state interference, finding expression for example in laws on the minimum wage. The minimum wage, however, is the policy implication of a mistaken history that we are rich now because the bargaining power of unions and the power of governmental regulation since 1800 have forced up wages at the expense of the bosses. If such a policy as a minimum wage worked as advertised it would be a swell way of driving up the wage paid in an exchange economy, or for that matter in a non-exchange economy, to any high level we wished, say $100 an hour. Let's do it. That we can't do it, and have seen attempts to implement it in places like Venezuela or "Red" China fail spectacularly, implies that something is wrong with the advertising.

The correct economic history is that poor people worldwide have emerged from $1-to-$3-a-day poverty to around $100 a day in the OECD countries because trade-tested betterment on a massive scale since 1800 has made many economies a great deal more productive. Then the supply of and the demand for workers, not power, determines the wage. (Minimum-wage laws, not irrelevantly, were first instituted a century ago, as Thomas Leonard has recently shown, to make it harder for women, blacks, young people, and immigrants to compete in the labor force. The laws have most gratifyingly succeeded, as one may see in the 50 percent youth unemployment in Greece and South Africa and in US ghettoes.[37])

An "unfavorable balance of trade" in Mielants and other Marxists largely innocent of economics, and also for that matter in people on the right largely innocent of economics (as again Donald Trump illustrates), is mercantilism, the notion that money is wealth. It is not. It is, well, money, good for whatever services in easier exchanges it provides but not the same thing as the food and housing it can purchase. If Poland's balance was "unfavorable" in the 16th century (later in fact it was not: Westerners had to provide Poland with colonial sugar and tobacco to make up the balance) it meant merely that Poles paid for Western goods with (say) silver, necessarily acquired by an exchange with someone else.[38] It doesn't make Poland less well-off by the trade, since Western workers and capitalists work to make leather goods and textiles for Poles just as Poles work to make grain and vodka. Both are goods. When they trade, both sides are made better off, getting goods at lower costs in other goods foregone than they would have otherwise. It's like your balance of payments "deficit" with your grocery store, made up by your wage "surplus" with your employer.

⟨≈⟩

I am suggesting that we don't want to prejudge everything about the mechanisms and morals of "capitalism" merely because we have defined it the way Marx did in chapter 4 of *Capital* (at any rate according to the standard, and inaccurate, English translation) as "the restless *never-ending* process of profit-making alone . . . , this *boundless greed* after riches, this passionate chase after exchange-value."[39] The original German, it should be noted, says "solely the restless stirring for gain, this absolute desire for enrichment, this passionate hunt for value" (*nur die rastlose Bewegung des Gewinnes. Dieser absolute Bereicherungstrieb, diese leidenschaftliche Jagd auf den Wert*).[40] Key words in the English translation of such passages, such as "never-ending" (*endlos, ewig, unaufhörlich*) and "boundless" (*grenzenlos, schrankenlos*), appear nowhere in Marx's German. The normal German word for "greed" (*Gier*), which most people would attribute to Marx's theory, does not appear anywhere in the chapter. Indeed, *Gier* and its compounds (*Raubgier*, rapacity; *Habgier*, avarice; and *Geldgier*, greed for money) are rare in Marx, in accord with his attempt to shift away from conventional ethical terms in analyzing "capitalism" and the bourgeoisie and the new world they were making—terms of disapproval that his favorite novelist, Balzac, for example, was more free in using. Marx's rationalist and materialist scientism, the intellectual historian Allan Megill notes, prevented him from saying, "Here I am making an ethical point," even in the numerous places in which he was.[41] The first 25 chapters in volume 1 of *Das Kapital*, through page 802 of the German edition (page 670 in the Modern Library edition of the 1887 translation into English), contain *Gier* and its compounds in Marx's own words a mere seven times (mainly in chapter 8, "Constant Capital and Variable Capital"), with a few more in quotations.

Max Weber in 1905, when the German Romantic notion that medieval society was more sweet and less greedy and more egalitarian than the present was just starting to crumble in the face of historical research, thundered against such an idea that greed is "in the least identical with capitalism, and still less with its spirit." "It should be taught in the kindergarten of cultural history that this naïve idea of capitalism must be given up once and for all."[42] In his posthumous *General Economic History* (1923) he wrote, "The notion that our rationalistic and capitalistic age is characterized by a stronger economic interest than other periods is childish."[43] The infamous hunger for gold, "the impulse to acquisition, pursuit of gain, of money, of the greatest possible amount of money, has in itself nothing to do with innovation. This [greedy] impulse exists and has existed among waiters, physicians, coachmen, artists, prostitutes, dishonest officials, soldiers, nobles, crusaders, gamblers, and beggars. One may say that is has been common to all sorts and conditions of men at all times and in all countries of the earth, wherever the objective possibility of it is or has been given."[44]

Marx, in characterizing capitalism in 1867 as "solely the restless stirring for gain," said he was quoting the bourgeois economist J. R. McCulloch's *Principles of Political Economy* (edition of 1830): "This inextinguishable passion for gain, the *auri sacra fames* ['for gold the infamous hunger'], will always lead capitalists."[45] But, replied Weber, it leads everyone else, too. *Auri sacra fames* is from the *Aeneid*

(19 BCE), book 3, line 57, not from the Department of Economics or *Advertising Age*. People have indulged in the sin of greed, a Prudence-only pursuit of food or money or fame or power, since Eve saw that the tree was to be desired, and took the fruit thereof. Soviet communism massively encouraged the sin of greed (which is Prudence unbalanced by the other principal virtues, such as Justice or Temperance), as its survivors will testify. Medieval peasants accumulated no less "greedily" than do American corporate executives, if on a rather smaller scale. Hume declared in 1742, "Nor is a porter less greedy of money, which he spends on bacon and brandy, than a courtier, who purchases champagne and ortolans [little songbirds rated a delicacy]. Riches are valuable at all times, and to all men."[46] Of course.

There is much, much more to be said about that old non-Marxist Karl Marx himself and especially about his Marxist-Marxian-Marxoid followers in the age of materialism 1890–1980, with their unintentional but nonetheless massive effect on killing off human flourishing and humans. The left and the right since 1848 and especially since 1890 have been holding, I admit, a mutual dialogue of the deaf. Yet as the economic historian George Selgin has observed, the main hearing problem in recent years seems to be on the left.[47] I do not want to be unfair to the rare exceptions, but mostly the left has stopped listening. In keeping with the simplicities of the early-life formation of political opinions, the left now supposes that rightists are simply bad people, who do not care about the poor and are therefore not to be listened to.[48] By contrast, the right is more likely to believe that the leftists are simply misled—not entirely bad people, though shamefully ignorant—and therefore that they might be open to patient factual and logical correction, supplied in bulk in the splendid publications of the American Enterprise Institute or the Cato Institute or the Atlas Network, long may they prosper.

Since the 1930s especially I reckon that the left has not been willing to listen to scientific correction. Karl Polanyi argued in 1944 that markets are new, but he and his followers down to the present have been unwilling to listen to evidence that markets are ancient. The Polanyists simply sneer ignorantly at the obviously bad people on the right who do not agree with Polanyi's conviction that market-tested betterment has been a terrible interlude.[49] Left and right have agreed that capital accumulation is the heart of capitalism—doesn't the very word prove it?[50] Yet the right has been willing at least to listen to people such as William Easterly showing that it is not.[51] Ownership of property, the left says, is the problem, and the solution is to eliminate it, despite the contrary evidence from trying out the program.[52] The left has supposed that "wage slavery" is a sensible locution, despite the logic and evidence that it is not, the putative slaves having been enriched by a factor of 30 or 100, and anyway not slaves by the definition of people who do *not* get anything like their marginal product, low though it might be in a poor economy. Left feminists have supposed that trade-tested betterment damages women, when it has in fact liberated and enriched them.[53] The left has continued to believe that socialism is a natural and indeed the final stage of history and that capitalism is doomed by contradictions, evident in every business crisis from 1857 to the present. The delight among my friends on the left about 2008, *finally* the Last Crisis, was palpable, evident for example in Bernie Sanders' charming revival of the deep thoughts he and I shared in 1961. Yet market-tested betterment persists and capitalism has not been doomed, spreading instead to China and India. The natural stages of history, says the left, need to be hurried along by (unnatural) assistance by the Party, because workers have false consciousness. But the workers accept a bourgeois deal and themselves rise into the bourgeoisie. The left has said in sequence, 1848 to the present, that capitalism results in impoverishment (it has not), in alienation (not), exploitation of the Third World (not), spiritual corruption (not), inequality (not), and, recently, environmental decay (correctible, socialism having done much worse).[54] Above all, the left has believed that economic liberty and social dignity, which were in fact the drivers of the Great Enrichment after 1800, expressed by the Blessed Adam Smith as "allowing every man to pursue his own interest his own way, upon the liberal plan of equality, liberty and justice," have hurt ordinary people.[55] They have not. They have saved them.

I plead with my friends on the left (and less hopefully with my enemies there), the loya followers of Karl, whose two alleged seats in the Reading Room of the British Museum I used to come early to occupy, that it would be good for them, and for the emerging prosperity of the wretched of the earth, to listen, really listen, at last, to the questions and objections. I want them, please, please, to consider what I myself have slowly come to realize since 1961, that Smith's liberalism, not Marx's socialism or its shadows in regulation, has achieved since 1800 a pretty good approximation to human flourishing.

Notes

1. But no women, dears—no Mary or Simone or Hannah or their followers are examined in our book. For shame.

2. Charles A. Beard, *An Economic Interpretation of the Constitution of the United States* (New York: Macmillan, 1913); Georges Lefebvre, *Quatre-vingt-neuf* (The coming of the French Revolution) (Paris: Maison du Livre Francais, 1939); and Christopher Hill, *The English Revolution 1640: Three Essays* (London: Lawrence and Wishart, 1940).

3. Hugh Trevor-Roper, *Archbishop Laud: 1573–1645* (London: Macmillan 1940; 1962), 3.

4. Learned Hand, "The Spirit of Liberty," speech at "I Am an American Day" ceremony, Central Park, New York, May 21, 1944.

5. Amélie Oksenberg Rorty, "Experiments in Philosophical Genre: Descartes' *Meditations*," *Critical Inquiry* 9, no. 3 (March 1983): 562.

6. Deirdre N. McCloskey and Arjo Klamer, "The Rhetoric of Disagreement," *Rethinking Marxism* 2 (Fall 1989): 140–61. Reprinted in D. H. Prychitko, ed. *Why Economists Disagree* (Albany, NY: SUNY Press, 1998). I recommend, for example, George DeMartino, *The Economist's Oath: On the Need for and Content of Professional Economic Ethics* (New York: Oxford University Press, 2011); Jack Amariglio with Deirdre McCloskey, "Fleeing Capitalism: A Slightly Disputatious Conversation/Interview Among Friends," in *Sublime Economy: On the Intersection of Art and Economics*, ed. Jack Amariglio, Joseph Childers, and Steven Cullenberg (London: Routledge, 2008); and Stephen Cullenberg, Jack Amariglio, and David F. Ruccio,

eds., *Postmodernism, Economics and Knowledge* (New York and London: Routledge, 2001). See also Deirdre N. McCloskey, "Sliding into PoMo-ism from Samuelsonianism," *Rethinking Marxism: A Journal of Economics, Culture & Society* 24, no. 3 (2012): 355–59.

7. Thomas Reis, cover, *National Review*, May 19, 2014, https://www.nationalreview.com/nrd/issues/376965.

8. See David Harvey, *Seventeen Contradictions and the End of Capitalism* (London: Profile Books, 2014); Immanuel Wallerstein, *World-Systems Analysis: An Introduction* (Durham, NC: Duke University Press, 2004); and Frederic Jameson, *Representing 'Capital': A Reading of Volume One* (London and New York: Verso, 2011).

9. Augustine, *De Doctrina Christiana* (397 CE), 2.6.40, http://faculty.georgetown.edu/jod/augustine/ddc.html.

10. Karl Marx, *Capital*, vol. 2, *The Process of Circulation of Capital* (1885), https://www.marxists.org/archive/marx/works/download/Marx_Capital_Vol_2.pdf, and vol. 3, *The Process of Capitalist Production as a Whole* (1894), https://www.marxists.org/archive/marx/works/download/pdf/Capital-Volume-III.pdf.

11. See Robert Nozick, *Anarchy, State, and Utopia* (New York: Basic Books, 1974).

12. Pyotr A. Kropotkin, *Mutual Aid: A Factor of Evolution* (London: Heinemann, 1902).

13. See Deirdre N. McCloskey, *Bourgeois Equality: How Ideas, Not Capital or Institutions, Enriched the World* (Chicago: University of Chicago Press, 2016), 47–48, 547–49, and especially pp. 579–83.

14. Eric Hobsbawm, *Interesting Times: A Twentieth Century Life* (London: Allan Lane, Penguin 2003). I knew Hobsbawm a little while a visiting fellow at the Department of History at Birkbeck College, London in 1975–76.

15. Bernard Williams, *Morality: An Introduction to Ethics* (1972; Cambridge: Cambridge University Press, 1993), 6.

16. J. Budziszewski, "The Real Issue: Escape from Nihilism," http://www.leaderu.com/real/ri9801/budziszewski.html (unavailable May 27, 2016).

17. Michael Ignatieff, interview with Eric Hobsbawm on his book *The Age of Extremes*, BBC Two, October 24, 1994.

18. Daron Acemoglu and James A. Robinson, *Why Nations Fail: The Origins of Power, Prosperity, and Poverty* (New York: Crown Business, 2012),

471. See also Hill, *The English Revolution 1640*.

19. Arnold Toynbee, *Lectures on the Industrial Revolution in England*, 2nd ed. (London: Rivington's, 1887), 87.

20. Deirdre N. McCloskey, "Getting It Right, and Left: Marxism and Competition," *Eastern Economic Review* 27, no. 4 (2001): 515–20.

21. Jack A. Goldstone, "Efflorescences and Economic Growth in World History: Rethinking the 'Rise of the West' and the Industrial Revolution," *Journal of World History* 13, no. 2 (Fall 2002): 323–89.

22. Eric H. Mielants, *The Origins of Capitalism and the 'Rise of the West'* (Philadelphia: Temple University Press, 2008), 35, note 78.

23. Ibid., 11n24.

24. John A. Hobson, *Imperialism: A Study* (New York: James Pott and Co., 1902); Vladimir Lenin, *Imperialism: The Highest Stage of Capitalism* (Petrograd, 1917); Immanuel Wallerstein, *The Modern World-System*, vol. 1, *Capitalist Agriculture and the Origins of the European World-Economy in the Sixteenth Century* (New York and London: Academic Press, 1974); Immanuel Wallerstein, *Historical Capitalism* (1983; bound with *Capitalist Civilization*, London: Verso, 1995), 13; and Mielants, *Origins*, 11, 17, 17, note 24. 18, 21, note 41, 30–31, 43, and throughout.

25. Mielants, *Origins*, 17, 21, note 41, and 45, note 102.

26. Ibid., 29.

27. Ibid., 18.

28. Ibid., 19, 21, note 41, 30, note 65, 32, 43, 44, 45, 156, and 161.

29. Ibid., 13.

30. Edward Cohen, *Athenian Economy and Society: A Banking Perspective* (Princeton, NJ: Princeton University Press, 1992).

31. Albert O. Hirschman, *Exit, Voice and Loyalty: Responses to Decline in Firms, Organizations, and States* (Cambridge, MA: Harvard University Press, 1970).

32. John R. Hicks, *The Theory of Wages* (London: Macmillan, 1932).

33. John Mueller, *Capitalism, Democracy, and Ralph's Pretty Good Grocery* (Princeton, NJ: Princeton University Press, 1999).

34. Mielants, *Origins*, 23.

35. Paul Collier, *The Bottom Billion: Why the Poorest Countries Are Failing and What Can Be Done About It* (Oxford: Oxford University Press, 2007).

36. World Bank, "Remarkable Decline in Global Poverty, But Major

Challenges Remain," press release, April 17, 2013, http://www.worldbank. org/en/news/press-release/2013/04/17/remarkable-declines-in-global-poverty-but-major-challenges-remain. I join you in being puzzled by the divergence between such figures and Collier's one-out-of-seven estimate. I think it is because Collier was speaking of the distribution by country instead of by individual. But the statistical methods strongly converge.

37. Thomas C. Leonard, *Illiberal Reformers: Race, Eugenics, and American Economics in the Progressive Era* (Princeton: Princeton University Press, 2016).

38. Klas Rönnbäck, "Integration of Global Commodity Markets in the Early Modern Era," *European Review of Economic History* 13, no. 1 (2009): 116–18.

39. Karl Marx, *Capital: A Critique of Political Economy,* trans. E. Undermann from the 4th German ed. (New York: Random House), 170–71 (emphasis added).

40. Karl Marx and Friedrich Engels, *Werke,* Band 23, S. 11–802, Dietz Verlag, (Berlin, German Democratic Republic: 1962), 168, http://mlwerke. de/me/me23/me23_161.htm.

41. Allan Megill, *Karl Marx: The Burden of Reason* (Lanham, MD: Rowman & Littlefield, 2002), 262.

42. Max Weber, *The Protestant Ethic and the Spirit of Capitalism* (*Die protestantische Ethik und der Geist des Kapitalismus*), trans. T. Parsons from 1920 German ed. (1905; New York: Scribner's, 1958).

43. Max Weber, *General Economic History* (*Wirtschaftsgeschichte*), trans. Frank Knight (1923; Greenberg, 1927; New Brunswick, NJ: Transaction Books, 1981), 355.

44. Weber, *The Protestant Ethic and the Spirit of Capitalism,* 17.

45. Quoted in Marx, *Capital: A Critique of Political Economy,* 171, note 2. I can't find the phrase in any of the online editions of McCulloch's *Principles.*

46. David Hume, *Essays, Moral, Political, and Literary* (1742; Eugene F. Miller, ed. Indianapolis, IN: Liberty Fund, 1987), 276.

47. Personal conversation, September 2015.

48. The recent extremes of not listening are detailed by Kirsten Powers, a lifelong Democrat, in her 2015 book. See Kirsten Powers, *The Silencing: How the Left Is Killing Free Speech* (Washington, DC: Regnery, 2015).

49. See Mark Blyth, "The Great Transformation in Understanding

Polanyi: Reply to Hejeebu and McCloskey," *Critical Review* 16: no. 1 (2004), 117–33; Deirdre N. McCloskey and Santhi Hejeebu, "The Reproving of Karl Polanyi," *Critical Review* 13, nos. 3–4 (Summer/Fall 1999): 285–314; and Deirdre N. McCloskey and Santhi Hejeebu, "Polanyi and the History of Capitalism: Rejoinder to Blyth," *Critical Review* 16, no. 1 (2004): 135–42.

50. Wallerstein, *Historical Capitalism*, 13.

51. William Easterly, *The Elusive Quest for Growth: Economists' Adventures and Misadventures in the Tropics* (Cambridge, MA: MIT Press, 2001).

52. Leszek Kołakowski and Z. Janowki, eds., *My Correct Views on Everything* (South Bend, IN: St. Augustine's Press, 2004), 14 and 25–26.

53. Deirdre N. McCloskey, "Post-Modern Free-Market Feminism: A Conversation with Gayatri Chakravorty Spivak," *Rethinking Marxism* 12, no. 4 (Winter 2000): 23–37.

54. You will find much more enlightenment on such points in Deirdre N. McCloskey, *The Bourgeois Virtues: Ethics for an Age of Commerce* (Chicago: University of Chicago Press 2006); Deirdre N. McCloskey, *Bourgeois Dignity: Why Economics Can't Explain the Modern World* (Chicago: University of Chicago Press 2010); and McCloskey, *Bourgeois Equality*.

55. Adam Smith, *An Inquiry into the Nature and Causes of the Wealth of Nations*, 2 vols., ed. R. H. Campbell, A. S. Skinner, and W. B. Todd, (1776), in *Glasgow Edition of the Works and Correspondence of Adam Smith* (Indianapolis: Liberty Classics, 1981), 4.9, p. 664.

About the Authors

Steven Bilakovics teaches courses on democracy, capitalism, American political thought, and the history of political thought at UCLA. He is also the director of the American Dream in LA high school outreach program. Before coming to UCLA he taught at Yale University, Harvard University, the University of Pittsburgh, and Christopher Newport University. He received his Ph.D. from the Department of Government at UT Austin in 2008. His first book, *Democracy Without Politics* (Harvard University Press, 2012), draws on the work of Alexis de Tocqueville to explain the democratic sources of contemporary political cynicism. His forthcoming book, *The Anxiety of American Dreaming*, analyzes the culturally ingrained pessimism—the perennial fear that the American dream is on the verge of being lost—that shadows this quintessential expression of American optimism and exceptionalism. He has also written on the origins and meaning of the modern work ethic, the rhetoric of crisis in contemporary politics, theories of freedom and tyranny, and the American founding.

Richard Boyd is an associate professor of government at Georgetown University, where he teaches social and political theory. He is the author of *Uncivil Society: The Perils of Pluralism and the Making of Modern Liberalism* (Lexington Books, 2004) and editor of *Tocqueville and the Frontiers of Democracy* (Cambridge University Press, 2013). He has published more than 30 journal articles and book chapters on the intellectual history of liberalism, civil society, pluralism, the history of political economy, and questions of membership and boundaries in liberal political thought. His latest project, *Subprime Virtues: The Moral Dimensions of American Housing and Mortgage Policy* (2013), explores the moral consequences of housing policy in the US in the wake of the financial crisis.

Ryan Patrick Hanley holds the Mellon Distinguished Professorship in Political Science at Marquette University. He was previously a Mellon Postdoctoral Fellow at Yale University's Whitney Humanities Center. His research in the history of political philosophy focuses on the Scottish Enlightenment. He is the author of *Adam Smith and the Character of Virtue* (Cambridge University Press, 2009) and coeditor, with Darrin M. McMahon, of *The Enlightenment: Critical Concepts in History* (Routledge, 2010). He is also the editor of the Penguin Classics edition of Adam Smith's *Theory of Moral Sentiments* (2010), the editor of *Adam Smith: His Life, Thought, and Legacy* (Princeton University Press, 2016), and past president of the International Adam Smith Society. His recent articles have appeared or are forthcoming in the *American Political Science Review*, the *Journal of Politics*, the *Revue Internationale de Philosophie*, and *Archiv für Geschichte der Philosophie*, among others. He is also the recipient of fellowships from the National Endowment for the Humanities and the Arête Initiative. His most recent book is *Love's Enlightenment: Rethinking Charity in Modernity* (Cambridge University Press, forthcoming).

Peter B. Josephson is professor of politics and chair of the department of politics at Saint Anselm College. He teaches in the politics, humanities, and philosophy departments. He has served as the academic adviser to the New Hampshire Institute of Politics (NHIOP), program director of the NHIOP's Civic Leadership Academy, and cochair of Saint Anselm's programs for Learning Liberty and Education in Liberty and the Liberal Arts. From 2012 to 2015, he held the Richard L. Bready Chair in Ethics, Economics, and the Common Good. He is the author of *The Great Art of Government: Locke's Use of Consent* (University Press of Kansas, 2002), coeditor of *The American Election 2012: Contexts and Consequences* (Palgrave Macmillan, 2014), and coauthor with R. Ward Holder of *The Irony of Barack Obama: Barack Obama, Reinhold Niebuhr, and the Problem of Christian Statecraft* (Routledge, 2012). He has written a variety of articles and chapters on topics ranging from the political thought of Henry Kissinger to politics and popular culture to religion and political economy.

Yuval Levin is the editor of *National Affairs*, a quarterly journal of essays on domestic policy and politics. He is also the Hertog Fellow at the Ethics and Public Policy Center and a contributing editor to the *National Review* and *Weekly Standard*. He has been a member of the White House domestic policy staff (under President George W. Bush), executive director of the President's Council on Bioethics, and a congressional staffer. His essays and articles have appeared in numerous publications including the *New York Times*, *Washington Post*, *Wall Street Journal*, and *Commentary*. His most recent book is *The Fractured Republic: Renewing America's Social Contract in the Age of Individualism* (Basic Books, 2016). He holds a Ph.D. from the Committee on Social Thought at the University of Chicago.

Harvey C. Mansfield is the William R. Kenan Jr. Professor of Government at Harvard University, where he studies and teaches political philosophy, and is also senior fellow at the Hoover Institution, Stanford University. He has written on Edmund Burke and the nature of political parties, on Niccolò Machiavelli and the invention of indirect government, in defense of a defensible liberalism, and in favor of a constitutional American political science. He has also written on the discovery and development of the theory of executive power and has translated three books of Machiavelli's and (with the aid of his wife) Alexis de Tocqueville's *Democracy in America*. His book *Manliness* (Yale University Press, 2006) was not a *New York Times* bestseller. He was chairman of Harvard's government department from 1973 to 1977, has held Guggenheim and National Endowment for Humanities fellowships, and has been a fellow at the National Humanities Center. He won the Joseph R. Levenson award for his teaching at Harvard, received the Sidney Hook Memorial award from the National Association of Scholars, in 2004 accepted a National Humanities Medal from President George W. Bush, and in 2007 gave the NEH Jefferson lecture in Washington, DC. He has hardly left Harvard since his first arrival in 1949 and has been on the faculty since 1962.

Deirdre Nansen McCloskey taught at the University of Illinois at Chicago from 2000 to 2015 in economics, history, English, and communication. A well-known economist, historian, and rhetorician, she has written 17 books and around 400 scholarly pieces on topics ranging from technical economics and statistical theory to transgender advocacy and the ethics of the bourgeois virtues. With Stephen Ziliak, she wrote *The Cult of Statistical Significance: How the Standard Error Costs Us Jobs, Justice, and Lives* (University of Michigan Press, 2008), which shows that null hypothesis tests of "significance" are, in the absence of a substantive loss function, meaningless. In 2011, the book figured in a Supreme Court decision. Her latest book, *Bourgeois Equality: How Ideas, Not Capital or Institutions, Enriched the World* (University of Chicago Press, 2016), argues for an "ideational" explanation for the Great Enrichment, 1800 to the present. An earlier book in the trilogy, *Bourgeois Dignity: Why Economics Can't Explain the Modern World* (University of Chicago Press, 2010), showed that materialist explanations, such as saving or exploitation, do not have sufficient economic oomph or historical relevance. The first book in the Bourgeois Era trilogy, *The Bourgeois Virtues: Ethics for an Age of Commerce* (University of Chicago Press, 2007), established that, contrary to the clamor of the clerisy left and right since 1848, the bourgeoisie is pretty good and that trade-tested betterment is not the worst of ethical schools.

John T. Scott is a department chair and professor of political science at the University of California, Davis. His primary research is in the history of political philosophy, with a specialization in early modern political thought. Most of his work in this area has focused on the thought of Jean-Jacques Rousseau, and his articles have appeared in such publications as the *American Political Science Review, American Journal of Political Science, Journal of Politics, Journal of the History of Ideas*, and *History of Political Thought*. He is the author of *The Philosophers' Quarrel: Rousseau, Hume, and the Limits of Human Understanding* (Yale University Press, 2009), which has been nominated for several book prizes sponsored by the Modern Language Association and the American Society for Eighteenth-Century Studies. He is the editor of *Jean-Jacques Rousseau: Critical Assessments of Leading Political Philosophers* (Routledge, 2006) and translator of *The Major Political Writings* *of Jean-Jacques Rousseau* (University of Chicago Press, 2012), Tzvetan Todorov's *Frail Happiness: An Essay on Rousseau* (Penn State University Press, 2004), and Rousseau's *Essay on the Origin of Languages and Writings Related to Music* (Dartmouth College Press, 1998).

Susan Meld Shell is professor and chair of the department of political science at Boston College. Her books include *Kant and the Limits of Autonomy* (Harvard University Press, 2009), *The Embodiment of Reason: Kant on Generation, Spirit, and Community* (University of Chicago Press, 1996), and *The Rights of Reason: A Study of Kant's Philosophy and Politics* (University of Toronto Press, 1980). She is also the coeditor, with Richard Velkley, of *Kant's Observations and Remarks: A Critical Guide* (Cambridge University Press, 2012); coeditor, with Robert K. Faulkner, of *America at Risk: Threats to Liberal Self-Government in an Age of Uncertainty* (University of Michigan Press, 2009); and author of articles on Kant, Rousseau, constitutional theory, and public policy. She has held research fellowships from the National Endowment for the Humanities, the American Council of Learned Societies, and the Radcliffe Institute for Advanced Study.

Michael R. Strain is director of Economic Policy Studies and resident scholar at AEI. His research has been published in peer-reviewed academic journals and in the policy journals *Tax Notes* and *National Affairs.* He also writes frequently for popular audiences. His essays and op-eds have been published by the *New York Times, National Review, Weekly Standard, Atlantic,* and *Bloomberg View,* among other outlets, and he is a regular contributor for the *Washington Post.* He is frequently interviewed by major media outlets and speaks often to a variety of audiences. Before joining AEI, he worked for the US Census Bureau and the Federal Reserve Bank of New York. He holds a Ph.D. in economics from Cornell University.

Stan A. Veuger is resident scholar at AEI and the editor of *AEI Economic Perspectives.* His research in political economy and public finance has appeared in leading academic and professional publications. His writings for popular audiences on economics, politics, and popular culture have been published in outlets such as the *National Interest*, *New York Times*, *USA Today*, and *US News & World Report*. He received a Ph.D. and A.M. in economics from Harvard University and an M.Sc. in economics from Universitat Pompeu Fabra. He completed his undergraduate education at Utrecht University and Erasmus University Rotterdam.